HELPING YOUR
TEEN
DEVELOP
FAITH

DELIA TOUCHTON HALVERSON

Judson Press ® Valley Forge

Dedicated to
Warren Willis,
who led me
as a youth
at the
Florida Methodist Youth Camp

HELPING YOUR TEEN DEVELOP FAITH

Copyright © Delia Touchton Halverson, 1985

Published by Judson Press, Valley Forge, PA 19482-0851

Unless otherwise indicated, Bible quotations in this volume are from the HOLY BIBLE New International Version, copyright © 1978, New York International Bible Society. Used by permission.

Other versions of the Bible quoted in this book are:
The Revised Standard Version of the Bible, copyrighted 1946, 1952 © 1971, 1973 by the Division of Christian Education of the National Council of the Churches of Christ in the U.S.A., and used by permission.

Good News Bible, the Bible in Today's English Version. Copyright © American Bible Society, 1976. Used by permission.

Library of Congress Cataloging in Publication Data
Halverson, Delia Touchton.
    Helping your teen develop faith.

    Bibliography: p.
    1. Youth—Religious life.   2. Family—Religious life. I. Title.
BV4529.H29 1985   248.8'3   84-17142
ISBN 0-8170-1046-7

The name JUDSON PRESS is registered as a trademark in the U.S. Patent Office. Printed in the U.S.A. ✠

Contents

71239

1

Adolescence: A Stage Rather Than an Age

Adolescence has become an ugly monster for many parents. From the time that our children are small we often hear the not-so-comforting words "You think you have problems now; just wait until your child hits the adolescent stage!" And so we build up a fear of the unknown. We wonder how to prepare ourselves for the "hard times", or we just hope our offspring will skip over the troubling years.

Adolescene is actually a stage rather than an age, and each culture, and each person in the culture, meets that stage at a different age and with a different degree of difficulty. The stage has something to do with maturity and much to do with reaching toward maturity.

Dr. John A. Larsen, Director of Consultation and Education at the Midwest Christian Counseling Center in Kansas City, Missouri, states, "Adolescence is something of a developmental twilight zone that falls between the dusk of childhood and the dawn of adulthood."[1]

Adolescence usually begins between the ages of eleven and thirteen and progresses at various rates. Some people may not complete the process until they are thirty-five or forty. The chronological age of a person cannot determine adolesence.

Physically, we mature in varying stages at different ages. In fact, this variety of developmental levels among youth of the same age is sometimes the very thing that makes adolescence so hard on the youth themselves.

In the struggle for independence from family, the youth look to other teens, and when they are physically developing slower or faster than their friends, they can have difficulty feeling good about themselves. Rather than thinking of adolescence chronologically, we need to consider adolescence as a period of transitional development. In fact, some people do not begin adolescence until they are about twenty, and some people remain in the adolescent twilight zone all their lives.

Today, with all of our media emphasis on adolescence, we often push our children into the stage before they are ready. From designer jeans for preschoolers to soccer camps for third graders, we seem to want our children to grow up too fast. In one recent issue of my neighborhood newspaper, I found pictures of fifteen-year-old drill-team members and horseshow competitors that could have been advertisements in a high-fashion magazine.

Not too long ago a group of adults and youth attended a conference in Europe. The youth attending from the United States were primarily older senior high students. Most college students in this country consider themselves young adults. To the surprise of the U.S. delegation, the European "youth" participants at the conference were almost all in their twenties.

When the death rate was high among children and our simple existence depended upon hard physical labor, society considered children to be adults as soon as they were physically able to produce young or to hold up under the strains of hard work. Even today there are some cultures that operate with these mores. Such cultures usually stage some sort of ritual of manhood or womanhood, and from that point forward the child is expected to act as an adult. Up until that time, children, lavished with love, usually spend most of their days in play or learning the physical tasks expected of them when they become adults. Any adolescent stage is short and is considered to be part of the time for children to play at being adults. There is no question, however, as to when the child actually becomes an adult.

Our culture has no such ritual, and consequently, for a period of years, our youth receive varied signals. They are too old to act childish, and yet they are not old enough for adulthood. They still need love and reassurance (which we all need), and yet they are working through the last steps of their journey to independence that they started at age two. They grasp every available opportunity to shout, "I can do it myself!"

Teens try to "prove" their manhood and womanhood time and time again—by reckless driving, by dressing to look older than they are, by staying out past curfew. Yet they still have a need to depend on parents. These struggles are the real tasks of the illusive adolescent stage.

Tasks of Adolescent Stage

There is no order in which teens face the tasks of adolescence. They will deal with one task and then another, and the insights they gain from one help lay foundations for the others. Sometimes we feel that the teens' struggles during adolescence are very self-centered. This is only natural because their primary tasks are to find answers to the question "Who am I to God?" "Who am I to myself?" and "Who am I to others?"

Who Am I to God?

Although young teens seldom dwell on this question verbally, it underlies the other tasks that they must accomplish during the adolescent years. The teen years are a time for arranging an order out of the disjointed experiences of God that have occurred so far in their lives. None of us are without memories.

We are learning now that even very young children have religious experiences. They just cannot put the experiences into words so that we are aware of them. Very few church nursery workers realize that as they hold an infant in their arms, they are laying the foundation for the faith of that child by giving an experience of love and acceptance within the family of faith. Belonging to the faith family, being loved and accepted, receiving a smile from adults who have no other reason to care—these are all a part of memories that the teen will fall back on as he or she accepts the unconditional love of God.

At one point I had a conversation with a mother who was a relatively new Christian. She told me of her concern that her daughter had not had a conversion experience. She said that her son was converted soon after she and her husband had been converted but that her daughter was very young at the time. Recently she asked her daughter if she didn't want to accept Jesus into her heart, and the daughter said, "But Mother, I've had Jesus in my heart for a long time now. I'm a Christian."

This mother found it hard to realize that her daughter could be a committed Christian without having had a specific place and time to point to and say, "This was when. . . ." She felt that her personal experience with Christ was the only route that was acceptable for salvation.

We each move into our understanding of who we are to God in our own way and at our own time. When a person has not been brought up in a caring, grace-filled faith community, then salvation comes about as steps into the faith. However, as G. Temp Sparkman suggests in his book *The Salvation and Nurture of the Child of God*, children who grow up within the faith possess a secure feeling that they belong to the church's fellowship and ministry. They need not ask for inclusion into the faith but rather are making steps of faith development within the faith. Salvation is already in process, and at the point of their believer's baptism or confirmation, they indicate that they understand the meaning of sin and truly acknowledge the working of God's grace in their lives.[2]

And so the Holy Spirit works with youth in various ways, pushing them into the faith or nudging them within the faith. There are as many time schedules for faith development as there are people. God holds the time schedule for the maturity of faith. The schedule is not the responsibility of parents, but we can provide opportunities for living on the growing edge. The person with a mature faith lives in constant relationship with God. The Moseses and Abrahams and Marys of our world have that faith. Jesus taught us the way.

Teens are ready to begin looking at their gifts from God. I have seen many plaques on which are written the statement "What you are is God's gift to you. What you make of yourself is your gift to God." If we can help teens to realize that God gave each of us gifts and abilities that are unique to each individual, then we have helped them on their faith journey. Sometimes this may be a simple statement such as "The way you are able to listen to your friend's problem with understanding is a real gift from God."

When youth can realize that they are created by God to belong to God, that God has a plan for them, and that they are loved by God no matter what (described by the old fashion term "grace"), then they are on their way to completing the task of determining the answer to the question "Who am I to God?"

Who Am I to Myself?

One of the hardest tasks for the teen is to discover himself or herself. A child's life has been filled with such close ties to family, community, school, and church groups that the drawing away to become an individual unto one's self brings apprehension.

Merton P. Strommen conducted a 420-item survey of over seven thousand young people in our country and discovered that the loudest cry of concern from the youth in our churches is a cry of self-hatred.[3] We, as parents, can help respond to that cry as the teens move through the task of answering the question, "Who am I to myself?"

A part of this task is to help teens to build self-esteem and to feel pride in their own abilities and contributions to the world. As Christian parents we can lift up their talents as gifts from God and thereby help the teens establish what I like to call Christian self-esteem: a realization that we are all important because God made us, because God gave us talents, and because Christ came to affirm the relationship between God and us, helping us to use our talents for God.

If you had eight children, what talents would you want each one to have? More than likely you would want one to be at the top of his or her class and one to have the kind of personality that everyone would seek out. You'd like to be able to stand at a sports event, swelling with pride over another child's accomplishment. Having a musician and an actor in the family would certainly give you a sense of pride, as well as having a child who was the perfect picture of health and beauty.

This question was posed to me at a parent/teacher meeting when our children were in high school. After we parents dreamed about our ideal children, the speaker reminded us that years ago most families had six or eight children and it was likely that every family had one child who had a great personality, one who excelled in sports, one who was beautiful or handsome, and other children who exhibited other qualities and talents.

Today most families have only two or three children—*but* as parents we still want to be able to have pride in a star ballplayer, a beauty queen, a child who makes all As, and a child who carries on our talents or exhibits the talents we wish we had developed. The speaker suggested that much of what we think of as teen peer pressure today is actually parent pressure. We fear that we will be looked upon as poor parents if we haven't given our children all of the opportunities to excel. We parents are satisfying our own needs through our children, and we load pressures on our two or three children by expecting them to give us the satisfactions that larger families of children gave to parents of past generations.

It is important that our teens begin to realize where their talents lie and make use of them. But we, as parents, must be open to allowing the teens to work with God in establishing those talents and not insist that they participate in all of the "cultural advantages" available to them. A part of the teen's task of discovering himself or herself is to explore various avenues, learn from mistakes, and appreciate talents when they emerge.

In John 10:10 Jesus states: "I have come in order that you may have life—life in all its fullness" (TEV). Recognizing God's unconditional love or grace and living in a loving relationship with God gives life a fullness that other people may never know. This relationship with God naturally leads to service to others.

A part of the pride a teen develops lies in finding a satisfaction in the ways that his or her talents can be used for others.

Who Am I to Others?

Concentrating on others expands the world of the teen. It is through ministry to others that the teen develops self-worth.

When we see the joy in the faces of those to whom we minister, then we realize our own importance to God.

You see, the tasks are all related and move in a continual circle. God made us and gave us talents. The talents are ways that we can share ourselves and God with others. The satisfaction and happiness that others draw from our ministry gives us self-worth and glorifies God. We move back around the circle to realize how we are important because of God's gift of ministry.

Throughout the process we realize that sometimes we fail to live up to our potential, but at that time God's grace (loving us no matter what) is always there for us to accept. We're important enough for God to love even when we make mistakes. And the importance and joy over that grace excites us again to use our talents for others.

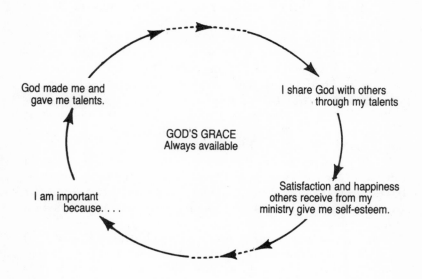

As our teens begin to develop their gifts from God, establish an understanding of themselves, and share their talents with others, they begin to sever the nurturing cord through which we fed them for years. They are ready to break away. Our teens are learning to recognize maturity as an independent, continual reaching to grow, the maturity that we have been preparing them for all these years.

Breaking Away

And so, adolescence has something to do with maturity and much to do with reaching toward maturity. The breaking-away process that began at the two-year-old's "I can do it myself!" age reoccurs more dramatically in adolescence, and we parents must realize that we have brought them up to let them go.

In Second Timothy (1:5 and 3:14-15), Paul tells Timothy that his background will be his firm tie in problem times. We parents may begin to feel the ache of uselessness as our children break away from the old ties, but we can realize that every loving hug, every conversation about a sunset, every hour spent together in ministry for others has been a foundation that will firmly hold our child's faith sometime in the future.

We may wonder about our teens when they are questioning the truths that we have held before them all of these years, but Jesus said that ". . . every one when he is fully taught will be like his teacher" (Luke 6:40, RSV). Most often, after the questioning, the maturing child will come back to the same beliefs that he or she grew up with through the years. And then the answers to the questions are part of the person's owned faith, not adopted from the parents.

Mark Twain is credited with saying, "When I was a boy of fourteen, my father was so ignorant I could hardly stand to have the old man around. But when I got to be twenty-one, I was astonished at how much the old man had learned in seven years."

In a high school commencement speech, Judge Rex R. Ruff of the Cobb County Juvenile Court, Marietta, Georgia, suggested to parents that they take the same stand with their children that the Juvenile Court Code of Georgia does. He said,

> In essence, it provides that a young person who violates the law, no matter how seriously, and comes before the juvenile court, has the option, after the passage of two years from discharge from the court, of having his records sealed. This simply means

that if, in a hearing, the court is convinced that the individual has not gotten into further trouble with the law, that there are no charges pending against him, and that he or she has been rehabilitated, the court will completely expunge his record. All past offenses are treated as if they had never occurred, and the court will respond to anyone making inquiry about this child's record, that no record exists with respect to this individual.

Judge Ruff suggested that we draw a parallel to our own family relationship. I would suggest that there is also a parallel with Christ's teachings of God's limitless grace when he told the woman who had been brought before him to be stoned that he did not condemn her and for her to go and begin her life anew (see John 8:1-11).

The breaking-away time becomes a time for the teen to develop his or her own individual identity. If we acknowledge that need, we are ready to move into a new relationship with our children.

This relationship acknowledges the grown child as an adult and must be established on an adult level. If we, as parents, recognize the personal selfhood of our maturing children, we will help our children to retain that selfhood as they move into the oneness of a marriage relationship.

Parenting Tasks

Like the developmental tasks of the adolescent, our parenting tasks during the teen years have no specific order of precedence; insights gained from one help to lay foundations for another.

1. We must let go without giving up parental responsibility, keeping a balance through the adolescent's struggles.

2. We model the faith, but we need not take all of the blame for our children's actions. We are no longer in complete charge. This comes as a relief, but we also begin to grieve for the dependency that is disappearing.

3. We develop a respect for the individual teen's emerging positions on subjects, even though we do not necessarily agree with them. We realize that this respect includes granting privacy so that the teen may discover the real person that God made him or her. We recognize that our teen is unique, that God made that uniqueness, and that the uniqueness is a gift from God.

4. We begin to come to grips with the parent's position in life—the mid-life stage when we move into the background away from our child and find other interests for ourselves. We develop our own growth as adults.

5. From this change develops the new relationship with our child; we are no longer superior and inferior but are gaining equality as our child becomes an adult with his or her own identity.

The parenting tasks during adolescence are in some ways harder than giving the simple yes and no of earlier childhood. But if we realize that we are in partnership with God in this process, we can move through the tasks and enjoy the rewards, discovering the adult relationships with our child to be a joy. We brought them up to let them go, and they come back as butterflies!

2

Communication Lines

"My teenager just doesn't say a word to me except to complain about the food."

"My teenager talks constantly, but I don't care about the things she talks about. Why can't she discuss something interesting?"

Whether the teen is the silent type or has a constant flow of teen talk that the parent doesn't understand, the communication lines are often broken for many parents and teens.

When did you last spend more than fifteen minutes in a two-way conversation with your teen without outside interference, not even the interference of driving a car?

When was the last time that you and your teenager laughed together over something? I mean really laughed until the tears ran down your faces?

When have you cried with your teen, sharing pain together, knowing that you both hurt and knowing how the other feels because of your own ache?

And when have you and your teen loved something in common and discussed that love? It may be a person, an animal, a thing of beauty, or even a common cause or activity.

These times focus on your emotions, and communicating at

a meaningful level involves sharing these emotions: emotions of happiness, sorrow, excitement, or dedication to someone or something you love.

Be Available

Communication with teens has been compared to catching tadpoles. The first requirement for catching tadpoles is for you to be available at the right place and at the right time. Running through the water and chasing after the tadpoles only sends them scurrying in the opposite direction. Instead, you need to find the proper place, the proper environment where the tadpole thrives, and be available.

Teens can make us feel that they really don't want us around, except to provide the physical comforts for them. Actually, this is all a part of their growing independence. They must try their wings. But there need to be times when the teen knows that a parent is there.

Even when our daughter was nineteen, living in an apartment, and working at a department store, we tried to let her know that we were available if she needed us. And there were times when she needed us. The payoff came later when she wrote in a card, "Thank you for being there when I needed you so many times this year."

One of the best ways to set the stage for communication is to provide some time each week when you are completely alone with your teen and he or she has your undivided attention. I'm not talking about times when you are driving to a ballgame or some teen function. Driving takes a certain amount of attention, even when there is no traffic. I'm speaking of eye-to-eye-contact opportunities.

Each morning at about dawn, a neighbor and her young teenage son walk by my house with their large dog. It is a routine time they have together. It offers them opportunity for conversation, and the boy knows that there will be a time each day when he can ask a question or share a problem with his mother without interruption from his sister, the telephone, or anything else.

Every parent can find some time each week to spend with each child. Make it a first priority for your time. Susanna Wesley had nineteen children. Two of her children, John and

Charles, were the primary movers in the formation of the Methodist Church. Although only ten of her children lived to adulthood, at least thirteen lived past infancy. And Susanna Wesley found time to spend alone with each child every week. Her dedication to private time that she set aside for each child paid off in the end.

Your private time with your child may be having breakfast together at a fast-food restaurant, or it may be lingering after a meal on a particular night each week. Your family schedule will have to determine the time. But the important thing is to be available, even if your child is not responsive at first.

Wait with Open Ear

The next rule in catching tadpoles is not to lunge at them when they approach. Instead, you must wait with an open hand and allow them to swim into your hand.

Teens are not always ready to talk. They are not sure about the environment. There will be times when you spend an hour with your teen and feel that it was a complete loss of time because no great revelations came about, no communication seemed to take place. But that hour was the beginning of a foundation, the start of a trust that will develop and suddenly open up if the time for one-on-one communication continues.

You may get fat on fast-food pancakes before your teen even begins to talk easily with you. But the time will come when he or she has something special to say that would not have been said without that personal time set aside.

In the meantime you can get to know your teen better. But *you* must be the one to begin the process by true listening. Too often we think of communication as a process whereby we convey our ideas to the other person and that person accepts them. Actually, *conversation* is what we're seeking with our teens.

Have you ever timed the amount of time that you talk in a conversation over against the amount of time you listen? A balanced communication will tip the scale heavily to the listening side. We need to develop the fine art of biting the tongue. There are certainly times to speak, but there are more times to listen in a parent-teen conversation.

Several years ago I spent some time as a teacher's aide in a high school library. When I first saw a student walk along the shelves opening one book, flipping through it, and then doing the same thing with another, I walked up and asked if I could help her. She said, "Oh, I'm just looking for a good book."

I suggested that she read the synopses of the novels from the book jackets that the librarian had pasted on the inside of the books' covers. Instead she gave me the criteria of a good book for teens. "I just look through the book for lots of quotation marks. I like a story that's full of conversation."

Real conversation is a two-way street; it involves listening as well as speaking. One good rule to follow in conversation is to refrain from speaking until you have listened without interruption.

There are two types of listening, passive and active. When we listen passively we hear words only. Often we listen selectively for what we want to hear. Or we listen in order to know what to say next. A conversation must be two-way. In fact, the best way to promote conversation is to spend three-fourths of the time listening and one-fourth of the time speaking, and let the speaking be questions or comments that prompt the other person to talk.

Active listening involves feeling the other person's feelings. It goes deeper than what is heard with the ears. In active listening we relate what is being said to a personal situation of our own, involving similar emotions.

Remember your years as a teen, not just the hard times when you had to walk to school, but the fears, hopes, and worries. Share with your teen what went well with you and what failures seemed to dash your dreams. Let your teen know that parents of teens and teens themselves are actually very much alike. There are only years between them.

In your conversations with your teen, be aware of the mutual feelings that weave a binding thread between your past experiences and your teen's current feelings. That's where communication lies, in the feelings shared.

Meaningful conversations are very much like catching tadpoles. If you jump at them too suddenly, you scare them away.

Be Alert to Opportunities

The third rule in catching tadpoles is to be alert to the opportunities. This includes the opportunity to pick up on what your teen is communicating even without words.

With teens, body language often speaks louder than verbal language. Be aware of differences in facial expressions, posture, and walk. Look for the situations when your teen seems to be more relaxed than others. Sometimes it helps to try to provide such situations or at least to be sure that you are mentally available for one-on-one opportunities.

A friend told me,

> I thought that once my child became a teenager I could completely forget about being available after school. Now I'm seeing that the after-school time is when he's ready to talk. He comes in and slumps on a chair near me, and so I not only arrange to be home but try to arrange any work I may be doing so that it doesn't require moving about the house at that time.

I've understood for some time that television can develop a communication barrier. It offers opportunities to be together, but that togetherness is deceiving. We are together physically, but we seldom communicate.

The dishwasher is another modern device that can hinder communication. Years ago families had the opportunity to communicate while sharing dishwashing chores. It was a time of physical labor but without mental requirements. There are few opportunities for this around the house anymore.

One summer we decided that both our son and daughter needed the experience of preparing meals. Each was to plan a menu, make up a grocery list, and then prepare one complete meal every week. I shopped for each menu with our week's groceries and was available in the kitchen as each teen prepared the meal. To my surprise, the bonus of the experience was opportunity for communication. As I peeled carrots or set the table and the teen prepared the meal, conversation began to bud. I realized that dishwashers and other time-saving devices had not only taken the place of time spent together doing menial tasks but had rushed our pace of life so that we did not have thinking time.

When I was a teenager, one of my own private thinking times was while I did my share of the family ironing. I actually looked forward to it, and usually did it with no radio or TV turned on. My mind wandered as I pushed the iron across the moist starched shirts. A hurried teen has no time to form thoughts. If we provide opportunities for leisure thoughts, then deep communication will develop.

Hold On Loosely

The fourth rule for catching tadpoles is to hold on to them loosely. Tadpoles can be injured by a grasping hand, and the same is true with new efforts in communication.

Try this: Spend a week making only positive comments about your teen's actions. Soon you will discover that there are probably more positive than negative actions. But I will give you a word of warning. At first you will have to look for the positive actions. It is not that the positive actions are not there, but that we do not see them. We have so conditioned ourselves to believing that our responsibility as a parent is to correct the bad that we ignore the positive and center on the negative.

One parent looks for opportunities to tell the teen, "You were really showing God's love when you did that." Another parent always thanks the teen when a job is done, even if it is an expected chore. Affirming the positive holds the teen in our love, but doesn't bruise the independence that is a part of the development of adolescence.

Listen to your teen without giving advice unless you are asked for it. And then let it begin with such statements as: "What are some of the solutions you've considered?" or "How would you like to see this problem solved?" The teen may state just what you would have advised. But if the solution comes from the teen, then confidence is developed in his or her ability to solve problems. After all, that's what parents are for: to help the children develop into confident adults. We don't have to solve their problems, only to support them as they work out their own solutions.

Complete Communication Breakdown

Sometimes a communication breakdown develops between you and your teenager. If this seems to be the case, try creating opportunities for communication, developing your listening skills, and affirming the positive in your teen every chance you get.

If there is a complete communication breakdown, then

professional counseling is usually needed. You want to be sure that the counselor you choose is professionally trained. Seek out a person who directs the counseling to the entire family. Find out if the counselor places emphasis equally on the individual and on the family relationship, developing and bringing out the best in the family instead of just pointing out mistakes. You will want a counselor who considers the problem, not as the teen's problem alone, but as a problem with the relationships in the family.

For the Christian family, it is important that the counselor and family share similar values. Many churches have trained counselors that serve a district or specific area and are available to the local members. Check with your minister about such an arrangement.

As you approach your teen about seeing the counselor, tell him or her that you want to find out just where you failed together. Where did the opportunity to grow together break down? "I'm not OK and you're not OK, but it's OK and we'll get help in working it out together."

3

Faith Growth Through Family Support

After forty years of wandering, the Israelites were about to enter the land of Canaan, God's Promised Land. In their desert isolation they had finally developed a community, a family of God. Now they were about to enter a land where other beliefs and worship of other gods would constantly be about them. Deuteronomy records two addresses that Moses gave the people before their entry.

The first address (Deuteronomy 1:1–4:43)reminded the people of God's goodness, the protection they had received during their journey, and the great land that they were about to receive.

In the second address (Deuteronomy 4:44–11:32) Moses gave a summary of God's laws, including the Ten Commandments. He stressed the importance of the relationship of the people with God and gave them guidelines on continuing that relationship, from generation to generation.

> Hear, O Israel: The LORD our God, the LORD is one. Love the LORD your God with all your heart and with all your soul and with all your strength. These commandments that I give you today are to be upon your hearts. Impress them on your children. Talk about them when you sit at home and when you walk along

the road, when you lie down and when you get up (Deuteronomy 6:4-7).

Our Hebrew heritage has given us a firm foundation for family support in religious growth. The Scriptures commanded that the faith be built into the family life pattern. When the stress was put on following the law rather than following the Lord, many of the family-support patterns for spiritual development became merely required routines and lost their meaning.

The routines and laws that Moses gave the Israelites were important for keeping the faith before the people. But later, when the laws were used as substitutes for the relationship with God, Jesus stepped in and at times acted in such a manner that the religious rulers of the day considered him a heretic.

Faith Memories and Experiences

Laying foundations in faith memories and experiences is important in the family's support of children and teens alike. In a faith-nurturing family, faith memories are begun early and continue through the teen years. We cannot "hand" our faith to our children. Particularly during the teen years, young people must be involved in creating their own faith. But we can provide the faith memories that will constantly be with them, and we can aid in that development of faith and be a backup when they need it.

As parents we need to be intentional about our faith, or we unconsciously tell our teens that faith is not important enough for us to share. In the past, society itself helped to nurture faith in youth, or at least it reinforced it. Lacking that support from society today, we parents must be deliberate in our support.

A faith bias gives direction to life. Often parents tell me, "I don't want to bias my child to a belief." Yet we carefully select schools, the language we use and teach, the families with whom we associate, the communities in which we buy our homes. Each of these deliberate choices teaches values and is actually a type of bias. If we ignore our Christian faith when we make our choices in life, then belief in something else will take its place. We might be teaching our children to believe in intellectualism or in "success" or in themselves alone.

We hear so much today about the importance of developing an independent child that we overbalance the scale on the side of choices and ignore the importance of commitment. In reality, a commitment is a choice.

Although a part of the teens' task of shaping their own faith is learning to make choices, they cannot be about that task unless they have some firm idea of what their parents' commitments are. Keeping quiet about a commitment usually signifies that we have no commitment at all. Consider faith as an intimate part of life. No intimate part of us can be shared unless we consciously do it. We often feel nervous and uncertain about sharing our faith. A friend told me, "The most influential thing in all of my faith building was the faith of my parents." If you have difficulty sharing verbally, begin by showing your commitment in your actions and then talk about how your commitment brings about those actions.

Persons whom I have asked about their memorable faith experiences are strong on the statement that regular church attendance contributed much to their faith. At the time, they were not aware of it as such, but now they say, "Because I was in the church then, it led me to where I am today."

Stephen D. Jones, in his book *Faith Shaping*, recommends that every parent ought at least annually to tell the story of their faith to their children at the level that they can understand it.[1]

Talk openly about your beliefs with those from your faith community who visit in your home, as well as with members of your family. These discussions will develop memories of adults who continue to grow in their faith.

Nature, and the opportunity to be alone, has always been important to me, although I did not consciously realize it as I was growing up. We lived in a very congested part of the city, and my parents were wise enough to realize my need to be alone. They made a concentrated effort to see that we visited a park or some other place away from the congestion of traffic and people almost every week. These are faith memories even more important to me than the sermons I heard during those years. These are memories of times when God was pointed out to me as Creator, as a personal friend who brings a soothing balm to the soul. When we were unable to travel to the less congested areas, I found a window that gave me a view of the sky and few buildings. I would go there and recreate the calm that was necessary in developing my relationship with God. Consciously unaware of what I was doing, I only knew that I had a need and these experiences satisfied my need.

The everyday opportunities to share faith that parents can provide for teens will develop some of the best faith memories. Celebrations of birthdays, graduations, major decisions, first fruits of the garden, a new home, and "first days" can all become faith memories if we celebrate them consciously as steps in our Christian life. A simple prayer to God in thanksgiving for the special occasion places it into the teen's mind as a faith memory.

Daily offer gratitude to God for the everyday needs that are met. Do this at impromptu times with a simple statement such as, "I'm thankful to God for this time we're having together."

Create traditions in your home. Consider ways that you have celebrated various occasions. If they worked well, plan to use them again. In creating traditions in the home think, "What will stick in my child's memory as a happy, joy-filled experience?"

Celebrate seasons, rites, and particular occasions as a family, and celebrate them with others in your family of faith. Make the home a place where Christian friends gather. Invite the pastors and others who have leading roles in your faith community into your home.

Think back into your own childhood and teen years. What are some things that might be labeled faith memories from those years? Think of highlights and one-time experiences, routine times, specific times with special persons who stand out in your mind, experiences that made a particular year a red-letter year, and deep personal times when you knew that your relationship with God was growing. Consciously create opportunities when your teen may have similar experiences. Although many faith memories just seem to fall into place, we need to be aware of the impromptu opportunities and deliberate about creating others.

Faith Clarifier and/or Advocate

According to Stephen Jones, every teen should have faith clarifiers and faith advocates. Usually the parent has been the advocate, as positive supporter of the faith, emphasizing commitments, stating a direction, and pointing the way. The timetable for accepting faith is the responsibility of the Holy Spirit. Our responsibility as parents and supporters of teens is to bring the faith—through experience, examples and love—directly to the teen.

Faith clarifiers open up choices for the person. They usually stand on somewhat neutral ground, lifting up dilemmas and ideas involving moral and theological problems. Discussion on the ideas and thoughts are encouraged, and when the teen reaches a decision, that decision is respected, even though it may not be the same as that of the clarifier.

As a faith clarifier it is not so important to give answers as it is to bring the questions to the surface. Then we must encourage quiet reflection when we can look to God for the answers. The Quakers call this "centering." There needs to be respect for the other's belief, on the part of the adult and on the part of the teen. You may not agree with everything that your teen says, but you can respect his or her opinion. Respect and agreement are not the same. Each person is at his or her particular place in the faith process.

In most cases a person can fill only one role, that of either advocate *or* clarifier. Then it is important that the teen have opportunity through the church community or other adult friends to relate to someone in the other role.

Jones stated:

> Young people are doubly blessed when the same person can be both a faith clarifier and a faith advocate. If a person has strong convictions but does not force them upon another nor insist upon agreement with them, if that person not only allows but encourages thoughtful questions, that person truly models the role of clarifier and advocate.[2]

Stages of Faith

According to James Fowler, in his book *Stages of Faith*,[3] our first experiences of faith begin with birth. He calls the early years of childhood a pre-stage of undifferentiated faith. By the consistency of those around us who are providers, we initially experience loyalty and dependability, two foundations for our concept of God. The transition to stage 1 of faith begins as a child learns language and develops thought and use of symbols in speech and ritual play.

Fowler identifies the first stage of faith development as "Intuitive Projective Faith." The child learns and develops by imitating. During this stage the child is greatly influenced by examples, moods, actions, and stories. It is a time of rapid imaginative development, occurring before the child can yet distinguish clearly between imagination and reality. Because of the patchwork nature of knowledge at this stage, children fill in the gaps with fantasy. Fowler suggests that most of us move through this stage between the ages of three to seven.

The second stage of faith Fowler labels "Mythic:Literal." It is typical of elementary-age children. During this stage the community of faith supplies stories. The beliefs and symbols of our religion become personal and can take on a literal meaning. When we begin to realize and acknowledge that there are different stories, we are naturally pushed into stage 3, a time of pulling the stories together and forming a conventional faith that we can believe.

The "Synthetic-Conventional Faith" of stage 3 typically happens during adolescence, when there is an upheaval in physical and emotional development. The adolescent works to pull the varying parts of his or her world together: the community, the school, the church, the family, and his or her peers. The person at this stage begins to form an identity, but the teen is not yet sure enough of this identity to step outside of himself or herself and look at it from an objective point of view.

Stage 4, "Individuative-Reflective Faith," begins when the person is ready to take responsibility for his or her own commitment and beliefs, looking at symbols with the question "What does it mean?" and asking of heretofore conventional beliefs the question "Is this what I really believe?" In this stage we look for logical and clear distinctions between varying beliefs, looking at them all and making decisions. The usual time for this stage is during the early to mid-twenties, but it can begin earlier.

In the "Conjunctive" stage (5) we begin to pull these decisions together into a faith that we can truly acknowledge as our own, and we are no longer threatened by others' beliefs.

In stage 5 we see faith as unifying; we are part of the faith but are still looking at it, examining it.

Stage 6 Fowler labels "Universalizing Faith." He believes that only a few in our world ever reach this stage. Those few have become totally immersed in the being of God and yet see the universal life as a whole.

There have been several studies of the faith process. Each one points out the definite stage of questioning that we must all go through in order to arrive at a personal faith, apart from the faith of others. This faith may be the same as before, but now it is separate. Fowler calls this stage "Individuative-Reflective Faith." Faith becomes individual, apart from others, and it reflects on the concepts earlier learned. The individual acknowledges the burden of responsibility for his or her own beliefs and attitudes. Sometimes this stage is hard for parents because the late adolescent begins to pull away from the parent and develop an individual faith.

Share with Teens

How many of us know all that there is to know about our Christian faith? We need to tell the teens this. Feel free to talk with them about any insights and new ideas that you gain in study or in your Sunday church school class discussions or in reading the Scriptures. Share the faith stages with your teens. Then they know that you understand their questioning and that you want them to reach a mature faith. A conscious acceptance and rejection of parents' ideas is necessary for teens to develop a personal faith of their own.

We, as adults, need to be role models—not of completed faith (because we will never arrive at that) but of a growing faith process. We need to realize that each person must work through his or her own faith process. And our major role as parents of teens is to listen, listen, listen to the teens. And then, above all else, to love.

Above All Else, Love

Love is of prime importance in modeling the faith. I have heard it said that every person needs to have someone who is irrationally crazy about him or her. Teens can grow through their teen years without knowing how to care for another person or how to give love that is any deeper than the satisfying action of a physical hunger, because they have never had such a love for them expressed.

We must keep our teens' emotional banks full. Loving teens is like building protective barriers along the road and teaching them to drive while they are on top of the hill, instead of building hospitals at the bottom of a cliff. A teen is more prone to fight and argue with parents and siblings when he or she feels inadequate. We need to love away their low self-esteem.

It is important that we show love for teens by establishing certain loving limits around the teenagers for their protection. Parents have told me how their teens developed a pride in the regulations that were set in the family, as long as they knew that these regulations were for their protection. We help the teens know from the beginning that we want them to mature to the stage at which certain regulations will be removed. If they realize that we are trying to help them reach that point and that we will tell them as soon as we feel they have reached it, then they will not resent the regulations. All along the way, however, when a point of maturity has been reached, then we must celebrate that progress with the teen and recognize that maturity.

Discipline comes from the root word "disciple." It is not a punishment but rather a following, a modeling. We model best, not by being perfect and expecting strict adherence to the "letter of the law," but by being more accepting of others, more compassionate and filled with hope and love.

Perhaps as parents and leaders of teens we should be prophets to our teens, prophets who can see through everything to the beauty of a person and love the beauty that God placed there.

I had a parent during a workshop say, "I think when I know how much I love my child and he loves me, I realize just what God did for me."

HOW CAN I LOVE MY TEEN?

Do I love my teen with IF . . . BECAUSE clauses?

I love you IF you are always neat and don't spend money foolishly

BECAUSE the way you look and act reflects on me.

I love you IF you make good grades
    BECAUSE that means I'm smart to have a bright kid.
I love you IF you are a star athlete or class leader
    BECAUSE I always wanted to be a hero in high school.
I love you IF you carry on an intellectual conversation with adults
    BECAUSE it will impress my associates.
I love you IF you adopt my religious beliefs
    BECAUSE I've found them to be right for me.

Or do I love my teen as Jesus taught, with EVEN . . . ANYWAY clauses?
    EVEN when your room is a total mess and your money is gone,
        I love you ANYWAY.
    EVEN when you bring home a grade that is not high in your class,
        I love you ANYWAY.
    EVEN when you sit on the bench or at the back of a class meeting,
        I love you ANYWAY.
    EVEN if you are shy in conversations with my adult friends,
        I love you ANYWAY.
    EVEN when we disagree in convictions and I think you're wrong,
        I love you ANYWAY.
        And I'll listen
Because love is more than looks and money,
    more than grades and popularity,
        more than intellect.
Love comes from God and is channeled to you through me.
    I know that you are on your faith journey,
        and I am on mine.
    We are not at the same crossroads,
        but we share the journey together.
And I respect your route.

4

The Church: The Supporting Family of God

During persons' adolescent years the church can be of primary importance in two ways: in providing a caring community that is centered in God and in helping teens sort through their own personal faith stories and memories.

A Caring Community

We of the church community must realize the role we play while teens are moving through their affiliative process of faith. The fact that we are chosen people of God, as Peter states in his first letter, is significant for youth (1 Peter 2:9). A community or group relationship is of great consequence during the adolescent years. The teen is in the midst of emotional growth that makes belonging to a group imperative. Coming to a sense of participation in the family of God parallels this time in a teen's emotional development and the development of his or her faith.

David Ng of the the Division of Education and Ministry of the National Council of Churches of Christ stated, in a seminar on faith in the family, that total church experiences, such as family night suppers, are important to the nurturing of faith. He said that his family usually gets to the church early for a dinner and helps set the tables together. But, he said, once the crowd begins to arrive, they seek other friendships among the members of the church family. His son may eat at the table with some other adult, and he or his wife may find someone else in the church with whom to share conversation during the meal. Ng feels that the relationships between different ages within the church family are of vital importance. Actually, there are very few opportunities for intergenerational experiences elsewhere in our society today.

Be alert that other adults in the family of God can be helpful to your teen in developing his or her faith. Seek out relationships with a variety of adult personalities, because one need of your teen may be answered by one person while another need may be met by a different person.

William Barclay, in *The Letters to Timothy, Titus, and Philemon* (a part of his Daily Study Bible series), suggests that Paul became Timothy's hero, even though Timothy must have been young when he first met Paul. Although Timothy had been raised in the faith, he found in Paul a surrogate parent of faith.

A friend shared with me his experience with a teacher he had in his youth years during World War II. He was a member of a boys' Sunday school class. His teacher organized the boys into a Boys' Battalion Prayer Band. Each boy was encouraged to write national leaders and tell them, "We're praying for you." To their surprise, answers came from the leaders expressing appreciation for their prayers. My friend's experience as one of a group of boys praying for a common cause made a lasting impression on him, and he is now director of religious education at an army post.

Our church recently had an exceptionally large confirmation class, a result of the baby boom after the Vietnam War. As I was planning the curriculum for the class and trying to share in the teaching, I constantly felt frustrated. It seemed that we would never be able to give all the important information to the many youth in our class and have them understand just what it meant to be a Christian. And then one day I was shopping in a large store and one of the girls in the class rushed across several aisles to see me. She had a friend with her, and her eyes shone as she introduced me. I realized then that whether that girl learned "correct" answers in class or not, the relationship with me as a caring adult would be a memory to last her a lifetime.

Rev. Bill Carpenter, a director of student ministries on a state college campus, spoke to a group of Christian educators recently. He told the group about a study on creeds that he led with his college students. He first asked them to write their beliefs on the board at the front of the room. He said that the board was filled with so many statements that there was not room for another word. Then he erased the whole board and asked them to write statements about their faith. No one moved in the room. The students began to grasp the difference between their faith and their beliefs. Finally one student spoke up, "Faith is the feeling of being humbled."

Carpenter suggested that we look at the Hebrew word *emunah*, which means total trust and confidence in God. This word is translated "faith." He said that we have faith for years but that during those years the beliefs that we claim may change several times.

Faith begins when the trust relationship is established between the person (child, youth, or adult) and God, and the foundations of that faith begin long before a child can even verbalize the word "God." As a parent establishes a trust relationship between himself or herself and the child, the foundation is begun. If the faith foundation is strong, then beliefs may be reviewed, rejected, or reaffirmed throughout life without a threat to the person's faith.

The Sorting-Out Process

During adolescence, memories and stories from past years are being pulled together in the teen's world. This process lays a foundation for the teen's own personal beliefs. At this time adolescents need someone in the role of clarifier, someone who can stand on neutral ground and help them to work through the shuffling and piecing process.

This is a natural role for adults in the church. Teens are in a position of creating their own world apart from their parents during these years, and often another adult can better fill the role of helping them to sort out and piece together their faith memories. This is why it is important to have a variety of adults working with the youth. Personalities differ, and we need to have several adults so that a teen may find someone with whom he or she feels comfortable.

Youth Programs

Youth programs in churches vary. Some are quite elaborate and attract large numbers of youth. Others are small. No matter what the size, the effectiveness of a youth program rests in how the program meets the needs of the youth in a holistic ministry.

Not only was Christ concerned that his followers read the Scriptures and pray, but he was concerned that their physical needs and their relationships to one another be met. His treatment of Zacchaeus pointed this out. Jesus saw how important it was for everyone to feel included in the family of God. What teen hasn't known what it's like to be an outsider at one time or another? The story of Zacchaeus speaks to the "outcast" feelings we all have had. Jesus was inclusive, and the church family needs to be inclusive.

I have seen churches that have beautiful youth facilities, complete with pool tables and video games. Some of these same churches discourage the teens from spending any time in the sanctuary outside of the corporate worship experience. In fact, sometimes teens are even "given" a youth worship separate from that of the adults. Teens can easily get the message "You are not important to us in our total church family fellowship. We have given you everything you should want. Stay in your place and be happy with all of the lovely furnishings we have been gracious enough to give you."

In their struggle for independence, the youth may seem pleased to accept such an arrangement. But an important learning experience happens when a teen worships beside adults, joins in visits at the church door after services, and is a part of the church planning process. In the relationships with adults, teens can see Christian growth and development as an ongoing process throughout life. They will learn that life in a Christian community is caring, struggling over decisions, and rejoicing in a growing relationship with God every day. Sharing religion with teens in the church goes beyond providing nice physical environments to developing common spiritual environments.

In our effort to plan a church program that will include the teens, we need to watch that we are not so "busy" in the church that we turn our youth off to the real meaning of our gathering as a Christian community. We sometimes fill the teens' lives with programs, and they are left deficient in thought-processing time.

As I suggested in chapter 2, the time for leisure thoughts is important. We need this kind of unstructured time in order to foster deeper communication, not only communication between ourselves and other Christians, but communication between ourselves and God. Television has fed our minds with words and pictures simultaneously for so many years that we have lost some of our ability to put together a mental picture from words alone. We must build time for reflection into our program.

Worship Services

Sermons and worship services also suffer from television's simultaneous feeding of words and pictures. The primary portions of our worship services are strictly audio, and when teens have been preconditioned throughout their growing years to experiencing audio and visual together, they naturally have difficulty with the audio alone.

Many teens have been a part of the church-family worship experience for years but have had no help in understanding what is happening. There are two ways that adults can help teens grow in their appreciation and participation in the services. Together, they can look at the different elements of the worship service itself and interpret the meaning of these elements, and they can practice different parts of the service so that the teens will feel confident in congregational participation.

As a family, look at the bulletin from a worship service. There are action times in the worship service that we don't realize. We *pray* to God; we *sing* to God; we *hear* God's word; we *give* to God; and we *act* for others out of our love for God.

Each church has a somewhat different form of worship, but the explanations suggested below can be used as a guide:

Prelude - Music prepares us to worship God.

Introit - The choir calls us to worship God.

Challenge to the Congregation - The minister directs us.

First Hymn - We praise God with a song.

Responsive Reading - Together we read God's word from the Bible.

Affirmation of Faith - We say what we believe.

Gloria Patri - We sing praise to God.

Morning Prayer - We pray to God for others.

The Lord's Prayer - We pray together as Jesus taught us.

Parish Notes - We hear how we care for our church family.

Offering - We give to God.

Doxology - We praise God for all on the earth.

Anthem - We think praise to God as the choir sings.

Scripture - We hear God's word from the Bible.

Sermon - We hear the minister explain God's Word.

Hymn of Dedication - We dedicate ourselves (promise) to do God's work.

Benediction - The minister sends us out to care for others and act for God.

Postlude - Music plays as we leave.

Since the early days of Christendom, most worship services have been divided into four sections, corresponding to Isaiah's worship experience described in Isaiah 6:1-10.

Adoration	Saying to God, "We praise you."	Isaiah 6:1-4
Confession	Saying to God we are sorry.	Isaiah 6:5
Proclamation	Minister and choir explaining God's Word.	Isaiah 6:6-8
Dedication	Dedicating ourselves to follow God's plan.	Isaiah 6:9-10

Another way to look at the form of worship is to consider each part and find the times during the service when we are talking to God and the times when God is talking to us, either privately or through those leading the service.

Borrow or purchase a hymnal that you use in the worship service and study the format of the book. Look at the indexes and become familiar with finding various parts. Take time to learn creeds and responses that your church uses regularly. One helpful method is to make a tape recording of these and practice them at home or while you are traveling, if you have a tape player in your car.

Teens want to be a part of the church family, and being familiar with all elements of the service helps them to be full participants. After participating in a worship study that our church conducted and after practicing at home using a tape recording, a boy told his mother, "Now I can say what I used to pretend to know." The boy wanted to be a part of the experience, but we had failed to give him the background and practice. Too often we expect children and teens to "catch" automatically our love and appreciation for the community worship experience merely from exposure.

James J. DiGiecomo, S.J., an assistant adjunct professor of religion and religious education at Fordham University, told of a time when he celebrated Mass for a group of students that he also had in a classroom situation. The students did not like his service, although he thought he had made them feel a part of the worship experience. When he asked them what they did not like, the complaints indicated that his style of celebration was what he called "vertical."

In his article "The Religious Needs of Teens"[1] DiGiecomo speaks of God as both vertical and horizontal, or transcendent and immanent. As adults we have learned to use certain attitudes in our worship. We create an atmosphere for our religious experiences by assuming a "holy" attitude, making bodily gestures of kneeling or bowing our heads, and exhibiting an almost forboding awareness of the presence of God. DiGiecomo reminds us that these attitudes are legitimate, relating to God as vertical or transcendent. There is a feeling of awe in all that God has done for us and in the mighty power that is God's.

But, says DiGiecomo, God is not only over and above reality; God is at the very heart of reality. This is the horizontal or immanent element of God that is important to teens and can help adults too. When God came in Christ, then we were given reality. This brought God to our own level, and we can therefore meet the Lord in one another.

Both elements of God are important, and our church community worships and prays together most effectively when we make an effort to combine the two, the vertical and the horizontal.

Steps Within the Faith

George Albert Coe, who helped revolutionize the thinking of Christian education during the first quarter of this century, spoke of steps *within*, rather than *into*, the faith. Prior to this century much stress was put on preparing a child for accepting salvation rather than helping the child to grow up in the faith and to understand salvation. Because of the scare tactics that had been used with children, the pendulum swung in the opposite direction. We became complacent about communicating the meanings of the rites and rituals when we introduced them to children.

Give a young child a set of watercolors and watch the discovery process. The child will put a dab of red and a dab of yellow on the paper. As the colors are stirred together, they each take on a part of the other, and suddenly a cry of joy will come from the child, "Look what happened! I just made orange!"

That child has had an experience of creation. It is a theological experience, at the child's stage of development, equal to a seminary student's sudden understanding of a great theologian. We need to celebrate every step and process that we go through in our development of faith. Let's celebrate orange!

Sacraments, Rites, and Rituals

Depending upon the denomination, baptism or some form of dedication of the infant is usually the first formal presentation of the child to the church family. This serves as the acknowledged beginning of the child's faith journey, although he or she has been surrounded by the Christian love of parents from birth. The child is a part of the love of the church family, and the family recognizes this.

At this beginning rite for infants, each member of the church family may celebrate a renewal in the faith journey, remembering the past and thanking God for those who prepared the path and established the memories.

Usually sometime between ages five and seven, the child begins attending worship services. There should be some sort of worship readiness training and then a celebration of this step that the child has taken in his or her faith journey. Some churches may mark this with a first Communion for the child, or perhaps this is the time to give the child a Bible or personal hymnal. However it is celebrated, the occasion is a marked recognition that from this point the child will participate regularly in the worship service with adults.

During the years between early elementary and adulthood there are two natural times for celebration in our faith journeys. One of these is when an individual person becomes aware of God's gifts, the gifts of the spirit. This occurs when we develop our self-esteem and our pride in the fact that we are modeled after God and that we are given talents to be used in the honor of God.

The time when the person realizes his or her talents as gifts from God and publicly uses those talents cannot be set by age because this recognition comes to different people at different times. A church may establish a workshop in which children or early teens explore their gifts and, at the close of the workshop, dedicate these gifts to God in a celebration service. Participants may be recognized as individuals or as a group, but unfortunately this important milestone for youth is often overlooked. We need to realize that this new awareness is an important acknowledgement for teens, and we need to celebrate with them.

The other important step in a teen's faith journey is usually celebrated as believer's baptism or confirmation. For the churches that practice infant baptism, confirmation also includes reaffirming the vows that were taken for the person at his or her baptism. The age of believer's baptism can vary, from church to church and from person to person. It varies depending on the meaning that we place on the ritual, and it varies depending on the development of each individual's faith.

But it is important that some special celebrative rite be accepted as recognition of religious awareness and awakening of a personal ownership in the faith. Those teens who have grown up in the faith may not need to "throw off the old life of sin and take on a new one of faith," but they do need to look for a response time, a time when they say, "Yes, I will declare the faith myself!"

G. Temp Sparkman, in his book, *The Salvation and Nurture of the Child of God*, says of salvation:

Just as we participate in the sinful condition of humanity before we understand its import, so do we participate in salvation before we can appreciate its full meaning. If evil can work in us prior to our knowledge and responsibility, so can the holy. However, at some time in our lives we come to face the fact of the division within ourselves, among our brothers and sisters in the race, and between us and God. In facing that, we are called upon to act on that knowledge in light of the work of Jesus the Christ. If we act in faith, then we set ourselves consciously on a journey which had its beginnings long before we were aware; in short, we allow God to work in transforming our lives or in reforming us after the image.[2]

We sometimes panic when we feel that our teen has not made a commitment to God. That commitment, however, is not our responsibility. It is God's. Our responsibility has been and still is to listen and to share our own faith.

The believer's baptism or confirmation of teens indicates that they have faced the meaning of sin and have some understanding of God's grace. This is the time when they themselves declare their own faith.

Adult Celebrations

We have put so much emphasis on salvation and becoming a full participant in the faith that we often give teens the impression that our faith development stops when we make the public confession of our sins and determine to lead a new life in Christ. It is important that as adults we reaffirm our own commitments from time to time and that we celebrate other milestones in our faith journey. One of these times is the launching of our vocational ministry for Christ.

As I was growing up, many young people made decisions for "full-time Christian service" while they were attending youth camps. This meant that they had decided to go into careers or vocations paid by the church. Gradually we began to realize that this term was exclusive. If, however, we are true followers of Christ, we should be in service to him in every area of our life, our career life included. In that sense we should be in "full-time Christian service" no matter what our career, and our choice of career should take this into consideration. As young adults decide on a career and become established in it, then celebration of their choice can be a milestone in their faith journey.

We are discovering that the time between ages forty and fifty is very crucial in adult life. Heretofore, many women found a lifetime career within the home. In the world of today they are encouraged to take a look at their lives and consider another direction as they approach forty. This requires a re-direction of ministry or vocation.

Men and women in their late thirties and in their forties who have established careers outside the home often find that technology has changed their fields or that their advancement in their careers has put them in positions they would like to change. At this time a celebration of renewal or redirection of ministry can help both adults and teens to realize that career choices are a part of a total Christian life and that we continue to move along our faith journey throughout our lives.

Retirement can be another time of celebration in our faith journey. The free time available to adults during their retirement can open up new ministries that were not possible while they were supporting a family. Recognizing this within the church family, helping people find new direction, and celebrating that time as a step in our faith journey again tells youth, "This Christian commitment is a lifelong growing experience."

One in the Spirit

Supporting a teen through the church means giving him or her a Christ-centered peer group and a feeling of being included in the family of God. Moses followed God's command in assembling all of the people—men, women, and children (Deuteronomy 31:12). Peter acclaimed the need of the people to consider themselves the Chosen People, a people belonging to God.

> But you are a chosen people, a royal priesthood, a holy nation, a people belonging to God, that you may declare the praises of him who called you out of darkness into his wonderful light. Once you were not a people, but now you are the people of God; once you had not received mercy, but now you have received mercy (1 Peter 2:9-10).

The Development of Personal Devotions and Study

When God revealed the name *Yahweh* ("I am who I am") to Moses it was a personal and intimate thing to do. The early Hebrews held God's name in such reverence that they did not even speak it aloud. Moses had spent much time in reflection as he tended sheep in Midian. It was out of this reflective time that his relationship with God developed.

When God told Moses to deliver the Israelites from Egypt, Moses asked what name he should use for God. The answer came: "I am who I am" (Exodus 3:14) or *Yahweh*. The most-used translation of *Yahweh* is "LORD." The revelation of God's name to the Israelites made them special, and that revelation came through the personal time that Moses spent in the presence of God.

God revealed divine attributes to us progressively throughout the Bible. Christ was the climax of that revelation. By coming as human, God experienced all, living through human trials in human form. Jesus was truly human, with human experiences; and he was also truly divine. Therefore we can be personal with God, through Jesus.

Personal God

Dr. Millie Goodson, professor of Christian education at Scarritt College for Christian Workers, tells of her niece's version of the Lord's Prayer: "Our Father, who aren't in heaven, how do you know my name?"

We want our teens to grow in a devotional experience with God that is personal. We want them to be aware that God knows their names.

If you have an acquaintance with whom you would like to develop a close friendship, how can you help that to come about? There is a little book on friendship called *Whobody There?* It speaks of "anybodies" and "whobodies." The "whobodies" aren't just anybody; the "whobodies" are special.

This is the sort of special relationship we want our teens to develop with God. We want them to feel that God is their utmost friend. In Matthew 10:37, Jesus said, "Anyone who loves his father or mother more than me is not worthy of me; anyone who loves his son or daughter more than me is not worthy of me."

We want teens to come to realize that God is foremost in their lives, not with a sense of fear but with love. This love for God does not crowd out other love for parents, siblings, and friends, but, instead, it makes that love possible. When we develop a deep love for God, then the love and concern for others comes naturally.

At the end of *Whobody There?* ideas are given on how "anybodies" get to be "whobodies." The first advice is to wait. "You can't hurry things like that."[1]

When we read John 10:10 in the first chapter of this book, we learned that Jesus told the Pharisees that he came so we might have life in its fullness. Jesus was speaking of fullness, not busyness. He wanted us to have a living, loving relationship with a personal God. We need to release some time for teens so that they can develop an awareness of the fullness of which John wrote and Jesus spoke.

We cannot develop a relationship with a friend without setting specific times for communicating and sharing. This requires discipline. The word "discipline" comes from the same stem as the word "disciple." By becoming a disciple we allow another to guide and direct our words and actions because we believe that the person to whom we are a disciple knows more about life than we do. As Christians we strive for self-discipline, in ourselves and in others. We want to learn to behave in the ways that Jesus taught us, allowing Jesus to control our lives.

Prayer and a personal devotional life can provide the discipline that will help us to grow toward the "whobody" relationship with God that we want as Christians. We cannot force our teens into this discipline, but we can lead the way. We can clear some of the busyness from our own lives and spend time alone. In quietness, study, and prayer, we can develop the "whobody" relationship with God.

Our actions and patterns of living are noticed by our children, whether we are aware of it or not. A friend of mine told me that her child notices the times when she is frenzied and out of touch with the Lord. The teen will say to her, "Mom, you need a prayer."

Whobody There? also suggests that the "anybodies" look at each other. The story is told of a preacher who looked up from his sermon writing one day to see his son sitting at his feet and staring at him. He asked the boy what he wanted, and the boy replied, "I don't want nuffin'. I'se only looking at you and lovin' you!"[2] In order to develop the "whobody" relationship with God, we all need to spend time just looking at and loving God.

This "looking and loving" is the first and foremost part of prayer. And prayer is at the heart of our personal devotions.

Prayer

It has been suggested that the word "ACTS" is a good word to remember in prayer. It covers four elements that are important in our prayer life.

Adoration
Confession
Thanksgiving
Supplication

Adoration

Adoration prepares the way for all else that follows in prayer. Before God came in human form as Christ, we trembled in awe of the mysteries of the universe. This reverential awe of the holiness and majesty of God is expressed in the Bible as the fear of the Lord. Our modern use of the word "fear" carries tones of panic and punishment.

Adoration goes beyond admiration or even awe. We can admire something or stand in awe of it without love. In our adoration for God we can recognize that through God the potential greatness waiting in each of us can be revealed. Adoration is not loving God because . . . , but loving God— period. It's just looking and loving.

Adoration in prayer is different from reflection. Reflection is the fixing of the mind on some subject. Adoration puts the whole self into the act, not just the mind. Adoration comes from the depths within, the part of us that is not explainable through science. Adoration lets our whole being go to the One whom we adore—God. It is through adoration that we prepare ourselves for the other elements of Christian prayer. Adoration is the foundation for confession, thanksgiving, and supplication.

Confession

Confession is meeting God and accepting the real truth about ourselves. After adoration has opened us to a loving relationship with God, we can allow ourselves to feel confident enough to confess all and to be set free by the truth of our real selves.

We can help teens work with their inner confessions to God by changing the wording of some of our attitudes or actions. In our childhood many of us were told that certain actions or attitudes were "wrong" or were "sins." Bishop Lance Webb, in his book *The Art of Personal Prayer*, suggests that we confuse sins with symptoms of sins. We will confess and ask for forgiveness for losing our temper, but we do not dig down to the reason behind the loss of temper. The reason may be a stubborn attitude about having things our own way. Confession of the symptom is important, but we must recognize it as a symptom and then look deeper for the sin. Bishop Webb suggests that we look at the things we are most afraid of losing, and behind those we can often find the real sins of our lives.[3]

Feel free to speak with your teen about your own symptoms and sins. In discussing your behavior and the behavior of other people, speak of anxiety, worry, fear, and hate as symptoms.

It has been suggested that the one primary sin is a separation from God, severing the relationship with God. Martin Luther said, "Whatever you give your heart to, that is your God." Confessing to symptoms can be a salve that soothes the itch for a while, but it does not take away the allergy that causes the itch. Finding the true cause of the allergy and dealing with it is the only way to have long-term freedom from the itch.

A part of the ritual for the Communion service in many churches is the "Collect for Purity," attributed to Bishop Leofric of the eleventh century:

> Almighty God, unto whom all hearts are open, all desires known, and from whom no secrets are hid, cleanse the thoughts of our hearts by the inspiration of the Holy Spirit, that we may perfectly love thee, and worthily magnify thy holy name, through Jesus Christ our Lord. Amen.[4]

Christ's life and teachings were positive, not negative. He helped people to move toward a new life and not dwell on the sins of the past. It is important that we confess our sins, even though we know that God is aware of these sins. Consciously confessing our sins, we prepare ourselves for the relationship with God that we want as Christians. We are able to put the sins behind us and move toward the positive life that Christ emphasized.

Thanksgiving

Thanksgiving is a vital part of our personal prayer life. Young children will spend prayer time thanking God, particularly just before going to bed. They can think of every person, animal, and object, expressing individual thanks and stalling their bedtime. But by the time our children reach their teens, these reasons for thanksgiving seem to fade into the background. Acceptance by their peers, which is so important to teens, often hinges on material objects. Consequently teens seem always to be in need of something, rather than thanking God for what they have.

We can help teens by personally expressing thanksgiving for all that God has given us. Thank God for specific friends, for times of joy, for opportunities to help others, for the church family, for music you hear, for the beauty of nature, for a kind word spoken to you, for the opportunity to love God—the list could go on and on. In fact, you might begin a family log for thanksgiving. Post a paper at some obvious location in the house and title it "A Thankful Heart." Begin the list, and encourage other members of the family to add to it. The list may be used in both family and private prayer time. It can provide a good basis for litany to be used in the family.

It is through thanksgiving that we realize our gifts, become happy with our own life, and are able to extend God's love to others. The joy that comes from a thankful heart is the mark of a Christian. With this Christian joy we are able to enter into a creative partnership with God.

Supplication

Supplication is a word few of us use. A more familiar word is petition. But today our petitions are papers that we sign in order to try to persuade someone to act in our favor or in favor of something we support. This implies pounding away at God to bring about our own way. That implication inhibits our partnership with God, particularly any creativity in that partnership.

If teens have spent all of their lives praying "for" something to happen and fail to see it happen, then they will put prayer in the same category as requests to Santa and magic tricks.

Bob was a member of our church who discovered he had cancer. He was actively involved in the church. His wife attended and participated in programs, but she did not have Bob's dedication. Their teenage daughters were in the youth group. As Bob's fight with cancer progressed, his wife sought spiritual help elsewhere. She found a church that gave her a special formula for prayer and told her that with that formula and deep faith, Bob would be healed.

When healing did not take place, Bob's wife blamed it on his lack of faith and divorced him. Her church encouraged her to "rid herself of the stumbling block in her own faith." The teen daughters were forced to decide between their mother, who believed that she found new spiritual understanding, and their father, who was dying of cancer but could petition God for the help he needed to deal with his stressful situation, still holding onto the love that he knew God gives.

The teenage girls had two types of petition prayers, or prayers of supplication, modeled for them. The mother petitioned God to be on her side, healing so that she might have a physically whole husband. The father's petition gave him the ability to be in tune with God as a partner in his life. Even though the father was not healed physically, his petition released his body and mind so that he could be on God's side, establishing a partnership with God. He received the inner healing that helped him through the final months of his life.

I like to look at the creative partnership with God in petition prayer as a senior/junior partnership, in which the senior partner is conscious of the needs of the junior partner. But if those needs are filled without the junior partner's awareness of these needs, then the growth of the junior partner is stunted.

Praying a petition prayer must include our needs and our desires. Jesus' inclusion of our daily bread in his prayer model pointed this out. By recognizing our needs openly, we acknowledge our position as junior partner, putting us on God's side instead of petitioning God to be on our side.

The Lord's Prayer

Help your teen understand the prayer that Jesus taught his disciples in Matthew 6:9-13. Point out that the form and wording of the prayer that we pray in unison is from the first English version of the Bible that was made available to the common people. We think of the terms "thee and thou" as being reverent and formal. Actually, at the time of translation these terms were the personal forms of the pronoun "you." This makes the Lord's Prayer a very personal prayer.

Reading the prayer from various translations of the Bible can be helpful. A shorter version of the prayer is also found in Luke 11:2-4. If you can borrow several translations of the Bible, ask each family member to study a different translation during private devotional time and then talk together about them during a family time.

When you study the prayer itself, discuss the parts of the prayer that are adoration, confession, thanksgiving, and supplication. The first part of the prayer offers praise to God. In the second sentence we pray that all of us on earth will live as God wants us to live.

In praying for "our daily bread," we recognize God as the Creator of all the world, particularly of the physical elements that sustain life. The gift of food is a part of the dependable plan of God.

The word "trespasses" was the word for sin during the time of King James, when this English version of the Bible was first printed. Sometimes when we pray the prayer, we use the word "debts," which can also mean sin.

In your study of the Lord's Prayer with teens, help them to realize that we are asking forgiveness for all that we do to separate us from God. In asking, we know that we are forgiven if we are truly sorry. "As we forgive" indicates that we realize that we must forgive others in order to set ourselves in a right relationship with God.

By asking God to "lead us not into temptation, but deliver us from evil," we recognize that God's help is available for us and acknowledge our need for it.

The close of the prayer again recognizes God as forever over all the world, affirming the power and glory. The word "amen" is a form of thanksgiving and praise. It can be interpreted, "I really mean it!"

During a closing prayer circle on a college campus recently, a student used part of the Lord's Prayer in a personal way. He said,

Not my will, but Thy will be done.
Thy will be done.
Thy will be done.
Thy will.

Left Brain/Right Brain

Much has been written lately about the left brain and the right brain. In Matthew 22:37 (TEV) Jesus answered the Pharisee with the greatest commandment, "Love the Lord your God with all your heart, with all your soul, and with all your mind." The recent study of the brain points out how we have spent most of our lives feeding the left brain with rational and analytic answers and stressing rote memory, while starving the right brain.

Christ said for us to love the Lord with *all* of our mind.

Prayer using the left brain is verbal, rote-memory-type prayer.

This kind of experience is important. Saying memorized prayers has been compared to practicing swimming strokes on the edge of the pool. The practice is important, but actually getting into the deep water and swimming is like trusting a relationship with God that says "I believe that you will hold me up in deep water."

Prayer using the right brain is necessary to give us a complete prayer life. Family experiences of fasting (see page 59) or conversational prayer can help reach the right side of our brain. Symbolic, intuitive, visual, meditative, and holistic experiences in prayer feed the right side of the brain.

Conversational Prayer

Prayer for teens needs to be informal and conversational. It can happen at any time and at any place. Many times teens are in a pickle and need to feel free to call intuitively on God's guidance.

One of my most common prayers is, "OK, God, I'm here in this pickle. I know that perhaps I could have avoided this particular situation, but it's done now and I really need you to guide me in the direction you want me to go."

In order to feel free to admit our mistakes and call on God for guidance after we err, we must accept the grace of God— the attribute of an ever-loving God who says, "I love you anyway." You, as a parent, can exemplify God's grace by being supportive even when your teen makes a mistake, disliking the mistake but loving anyway.

When a teen has been raised in the faith, we might feel that by the adolescent years the person is well grounded and should be able to participate in verbal prayer spontaneously. In reality, at the time that we now expect them to launch out on their own in prayer, they are naturally self-conscious about everything. They not only don't want to pray aloud publicly but also are not anxious for their friends to know that they pray privately.

At this time it is natural that they balk at family devotions. If this happens, offer an alternative. Each family member may have devotions privately, using identical material. Then the family may be able to talk about their experiences while eating a meal or traveling in the car. The best approach may be simply to offer materials for personal devotions, state that you believe devotional time is important and you intend to continue your devotions personally, and invite him or her to do the same. Your example, not your force, speaks loudest.

Devotional Guides

Consider the whole of your teen as you help him or her select a devotional guide. Some devotionals for teens are filled with scriptural "answers" to dilemmas. Although these are useful in helping teens think through the beliefs of others, be sure that the devotional material available encourages reflective times, opportunities for their own "burning bush" experiences with God. Such experiences cannot come when we're hurrying. Personal devotions should help the teen grow in the faith experience, developing a deeper relationship with God. When such a relationship is established, then the teen will be able to answer the dilemmas and questions personally, in partnership with God.

Of course the Bible is the primary devotional help. If you have several translations, ask the teen to read some favorite verses in all of them and select the version he or she would like to use. Changing translations from time to time can give Scripture reading a fresh approach. Chapter 7 of this book gives more information on translations.

Provide reference materials at his or her level. Some Bibles have built-in references and begin each book with information on the background of the writer and the occasion for which the book was written. Bible dictionaries are also helpful to teens.

The most useful devotional books for adolescents deal with the everyday experiences of teens. Teens are concerned with problems of poor complexion, relationships with their peers and family, and disappointments in sports. Many of the new devotional booklets are in the form of letters to God, stating particular problems. These not only deal with the teen's everyday life, but they also help the teen approach talking to God in a natural way.

Teens' Doubt

There will be times in a teen's personal devotions and study when he or she will doubt. This is all a part of the inquiry that is part of faith development. In establishing a personal faith, teens must question whether certain beliefs are their own or whether they are only mouthing statements made by their elders. Most often teens will eventually accept the beliefs that their parents, as advocates of the faith, have shared with them. But they will work to clarify their faith during their devotional time.

Provide notebooks, as well as printed materials, and encourage your teen to record his or her thoughts frequently. Have them write in a private notebook, and suggest that the teen periodically reread parts of the notebook in order to see how his or her ideas have changed with new insight and study.

All along our faith journey we sort and rearrange our faith experiences. Adolescence is a time of creating order from disjointed ideas and experiences. There will be times when the teen feels that God is not a comfortable God because of the confusion in his or her mind. But the journey will probably lead to the true God. Sometimes our most important religious experiences come through a period of doubt and inquiry.

We, as parents and friends of youth, can best help them through these doubting times by keeping them in our prayers and offering a prayer for them to be open to God's guidance as they search out their own beliefs and journey in faith.

Sometimes I Doubt[5]
by Thom Schultz

Sometimes I doubt.

When things aren't going my way, when depression begins to sink my spirit, I wonder if God is really with me. I sometimes wonder if all my prayers have gone unheard.

Then when the doubt has passed, I sometimes feel ashamed. What kind of Christian would doubt the existence or wisdom of God?

Well, doubt has faced Christians for a long, long time. Even those who walked with Jesus experienced doubt. While witnessing Jesus' spectacular miracle of walking on water, Peter mustered great faith and tried this miraculous water trick himself. But Peter became afraid, began to doubt, and started to sink. Jesus acknowledged Peter's doubt and pulled him out of the stormy water.

One of the other disciples is best known to this day for his experience of doubting. After the crucifixion, Thomas doubted that Christ had risen from the grave. But Jesus really wanted

Thomas to believe, so he asked Thomas to touch his wounds. Thomas' doubts dissolved.

God wants us to believe, to trust him. He doesn't dump us when we doubt. He's anxious to dispel our doubts and help us grow in our faith.

And that's the interesting thing about doubt—it can lead us to a stronger faith.

Have you ever really looked forward to going somewhere with a special person? Can you remember watching the clock, waiting and wondering if the special person would really come? As your departure time drew very near, you may have begun to doubt the friendship of your special person. But then, when the special friend pulled into your driveway, right on time, can you remember that rush of joy, excitement and warm new faith in your friend? Your doubt had launched your new faith.

God wants to fill our "doubt holes" with faith—just as he did with Peter and Thomas. God probably won't call us to walk on water, but he's eager to show his presence in the things and people around us. Watch for him. Ask him for faith. He'll deliver. Your doubt will lead to new strength in your friendship with him.

6

Jesus: Who Was/Is He to the Teen?

A child is born in an obscure village. He is brought up in another obscure village. He works in a carpenter shop until he is thirty, and then for three brief years is an itinerant preacher, proclaiming a message and living a life. He never writes a book. He never holds an office. He never raises an army. He never has a family of his own. He never owns a home. He never goes to college. He never travels two hundred miles from the place where he was born. He gathers a little group of friends about him and teaches them his way of life. While [he is] still a young man the tide of popular feeling turns against him. The band of followers forsakes him. One denies him; another betrays him. He is turned over to his enemies. He goes through the mockery of a trial; he is nailed on a cross between two thieves, and when dead is laid in a borrowed grave by the kindness of a friend.

Those are the facts of his human life. He rises from the dead. Today we look back across nineteen hundred years and ask, What kind of a trail has he left across the centuries? When we try to sum up his influence, all the armies that ever marched, all the parliaments that ever sat, all the kings that ever reigned are absolutely picayune in their influence on mankind compared with . . . this one solitary life.[1]

A teen who has grown up in a nurturing family, hearing the stories of Jesus' life year after year, will have a good foundation on which to begin to explore just what these stories mean.

During the adolescent years the teen works at pulling together the varying parts of the Jesus story and finding some meaning in it. Prior to this time in life, the child has little ability to think abstractly.

No one can tell you just when a person will shift from concrete to abstract thinking. Most people do this sometime during their early teen years; however, the beginning signs may become evident in the preteen years. Often the change is sudden, almost as if a window opens and the individuals can communicate on a more adult level. It is exciting to watch the growth of a teen and see the dawn of abstract thinking. This often happens at about the ninth grade.

Historical Jesus

Even in the early teens, we can help our children grasp the historical Jesus. His trade before his teaching and healing ministry was carpentry. There were no power tools in Jesus' day, and so this trade required physical strength. A carpenter's livelihood depended on his physical ability to handle large sections of a tree, cutting them with handsaws to make boards and posts. Chisels and heavy planes required strength as well as skill.

As you consider stories from Jesus' life, relate the distances of the journeys he took to distances that you travel as a family. Bethany was less than two miles from Jerusalem, and Bethlehem was five miles south of the holy city. However, when Jesus traveled from Capernaum to Jerusalem he went approximately 115 miles by foot. There are two mountain ranges that extend from north to south in the narrow country of Palestine. Therefore, most of Jesus' long trips were on steep roads.

Locate a topographical map that shows Jesus' travels, and look at the distances he traveled through rugged terrain. The usual route from Capernaum to Jerusalem also crossed the Jordan River twice. He probably would have gone to Ginaea and then crossed the Jordan just south of Salim. Following the Jordan River south, he would have crossed it again east of Bethabara, just north of the Dead Sea. On one of his journeys he went the shorter route through Samaria (John 4:4-44). Although this was a shorter route, it was seldom used by the

Jews because of the antagonism felt between them and the Samaritans.

Talk to your teen about the modes of transportation during New Testament times, and try to realize the physical requirements of Jesus' life-style. Artists of the past often depicted Jesus with a physique so fragile that he would have become faint walking the few miles from Bethany to Jerusalem. But if you follow the journeys of Jesus in the Gospels, you will realize that he was constantly moving from one community to another. Traveling around the country and many times sleeping under the stars, he led a rigorous itinerant life that demanded a hardy physical condition.

Fasting

Jesus fasted during his forty days in the wilderness. The practice was more common in the Old Testament than in the New. With the Jews' expectation of an approaching Messiah, the custom was not considered as important in Jesus' time as it had been in the past. To help your family realize just what the wilderness of Palestine was like, secure actual photographs of this desolate area of Judea. The ability to endure such a wilderness without food indicated the physical stamina of Jesus. It is believed that Jesus also fasted at other times, although he advised his followers to avoid the Pharisees' custom of declaring their fasting publicly (Matthew 6:16-18).

Fasting is a practice to which today's teens may have difficulty relating. Some churches encourage people to abstain from some specific food during Lent. It is a physical way of reminding us to stop and consider the meaning of the season. An experience with fasting may also help your family understand Jesus better. You might eat one meatless meal a week and give the money you would have used on meat to a special project of your church or to a particular charity. Be certain that the reason for this is understood, and become familiar with the particular cause that receives the money. You might want to establish this practice for a given time (perhaps once a month or once a week) after you learn of a friend suffering from cancer, and then give the money to a cancer research foundation. It is important that the benefiting cause have some relation to the teen's life. Fasting is an experiential type of devotion and learning. The practice itself is not as important as the new awareness you gain from the period of fasting.

Why Did Jesus Come?

Jesus came at a time when the Jews were in need of a savior. They were under foreign rule by the Romans. Not only were they heavily taxed, but they were also given no opportunity to determine their own fate as a nation. The Jews were expecting a Messiah (or savior) and prayed for the time when God would send one. But they were expecting a Messiah who would bring them out from under the foreign rule by force and establish them in the world as an independent nation with prestige. Even the wise men's visit to Herod indicated that such an important person was expected to be born in more eminent surroundings.

But God chose a different type of Messiah. Jesus came into the world, born to a peasant woman in an obscure village. He began his life on earth as a truly human person, dependent on parents, as every infant is. The humble surroundings of his birth serve to remind us that God knows us all as human beings, no matter the circumstance in which we are born.

Jesus was a part of the continuing revelation of God, begun in the Old Testament. The author of Hebrews indicated this as he began his letter:

> In the past God spoke to our forefathers through the prophets at many times and in various ways, but in these last days he has spoken to us by his Son, whom he appointed heir of all things, and through whom he made the universe (Hebrews 1:1-2).

Yet, Jesus was greater than the Old Testament prophets. His revelation was more perfect because he was God's Son. Throughout his life, Jesus brought new insights into the old laws. One example is found in Matthew when Jesus quoted the law from Exodus 21:24 and then said, "But I tell you . . . " (Matthew 5:38-39).

In their early years, children accept the fact of Jesus' life as just that—a fact that occurred at some point in history. Even if we tell them that Jesus was God's Son and was sent by God, they do not understand the abstract concept of the Trinity. They may not ask why Jesus came. But as teens begin to piece together the stories and ideas that came to them as children, they begin to question why Jesus came on earth.

Jesus showed us how God wants us to live. His life was an example for us to follow. However, if we hold Jesus' life before our children as an "example" of what the child should do with the purpose of getting the teen to act as we want, then we are irreverent to God. Share the good that Jesus did with your teen. Then let the teen draw his or her own conclusions. Help your child appreciate Jesus' life. Encourage the teen to study Jesus in the Scriptures. As teens grow to appreciate Jesus, they will strive to follow him.

It is through Jesus that we have a better understanding of God and of God's purpose for the world. Through Jesus' life and death we are drawn closer to God. This is the true meaning of Jesus in the Trinity.

Trinity

The Trinity is a difficult theological concept, even for us adults. We worship one God, yet the one God is shown in three ways: God the creator, God in human form, and God within us. Jesus was the God in human form. Jesus not only came to show us what God was like, but, as I have heard it expressed, Jesus was God wrapped up in the skin of a human being.

I think it is even deeper than that. Because God came as Jesus, in human form, we are able to realize that God knows what it is like to be human. Through Christ, God experienced human temptations, human rejection and loneliness, human stress and frustration, human sorrow and pain. Because he suffered, we can have a closer relationship to God. We know that God has lived the experience with which we are struggling and knows that experience as a human.

Your family may find it helpful to read through one of the Gospels, concentrating on seeing Jesus' human experiences that relate to our experiences and stopping to realize that in each of those experiences Jesus was God.

Jesus Understood Emotions

Jesus was constantly keyed into the needs and feelings of those around him. He spoke to Martha, not with a reprimand, but with concern for her anxiety and irritation over having to do all the household work of entertaining guests (Luke 10:38-42). He told his disciples not to be anxious and to have no fear (Mark 6:50). He understood that they would have sorrow but that it would be overcome (John 16:22).

Jesus experienced anger that was sometimes laced with compassion. In Mark 3:1-6 he looked at the Pharisees with anger but was also deeply distressed when they were trying to find a reason to accuse him. In Luke 11 (RSV) Jesus responded in anger to the Pharisees, with "woe to you" after "woe to you."

The most physical expression of Jesus' anger in the New Testament came when he drove those who were selling animals out of the temple. According to the Gospel of John, he even made a whip from cords and physically drove them out, turning over the money tables. However, Jesus did not allow his anger to cancel out his concern for people. He continued to teach in the temple daily, even after driving out those who had degraded it. John records that Jesus counseled with Nicodemus (a Pharisee) immediately after the incident in the temple.

Jesus taught that peace will come when we center our thoughts, not on our own advancement, power, and prestige, but on the welfare of all of God's family. Throughout his ministry, Jesus showed deep concern for the underprivileged and unloved. He healed those who had leprosy and those who were blind. He cast demons out of the demoniacs even though no one else would go near them. He went against all tradition and spoke to the Samaritan woman. He invited himself to Zaccheus' home, and he affirmed the woman who was to be stoned for her adultery.

Even when Jesus was tired and withdrew from the crowd to get some rest, if the crowd followed him, he continued to teach and heal. His concern for the people was always there.

Grief was another emotion that Jesus knew. Grief comes with a loss, whether it is the loss of a person, a relationship, or an experience. Jesus lamented, or grieved, over Jerusalem, as recorded in Matthew 23:37-39 and Luke 13:34-35. "How often would I have gathered your children together as a hen gathers her brood under her wings, and you would not!" (Luke 13:34, RSV).

Help your teen realize that Jesus understood the process necessary in grief. Reread John 11. When Jesus first heard of Lazarus's illness, he planned a learning experience for his followers. Intentionally, he waited to go to Bethany, and when he arrived, Lazarus was dead. Although Jesus knew that he was going to raise Lazarus from the dead, when he saw the grief of Mary and Martha, he had empathy for them and joined in their weeping. As Christians we are assured that death is not the end of our life and that we will have greatness beyond death, but the emotion that accompanies grieving is natural and must be worked through, not glossed over.

Jesus Faced Decisions

The first major decisions of Jesus that are recorded in the Gospels are the decisions he made in the wilderness. The bottomless pit that teens have in place of a stomach helps them to relate to one of the three decisions that Jesus made in the wilderness. After fasting, he was naturally very hungry. He was aware of the divine power that he had and was aware that he could easily turn the stones around him into loaves of bread. Yet he chose to use only his human powers and endure the hunger pains.

The other two decisions that Jesus made during his time in the wilderness had to do with life directions. Teens who are wrestling over how to gain popularity or make vocational decisions can appreciate the fact that God, as Jesus, made human decisions similar to theirs. Jesus could have thrown himself off the pinnacle of the temple and had the angels bear him up so that he did not strike his foot against a stone. This would have been a flashy, attention-getting entrance into his public ministry and would have made the people sit up and take notice of him. But Jesus chose to develop his ministry through other people, in the everyday life of Palestine, along the roads and in the villages. He left the wilderness to choose the disciples who would work with him and carry his ministry into the whole world.

The temptation to bow down and worship Satan was met with, "Begone, Satan! for it is written, 'You shall worship the

Lord your God, and him only shall you serve'"(Matthew 4:10, RSV). Jesus, as a human, decided to worship God, although other directions might have been easier for his life.

Jesus Selects Friends

Someone once told me, "If all of my friends were exactly alike, I wouldn't need to have more than one. None of my friends are like you. They are all different. That's why I have so many. I like variety."

Jesus was a friend to all. One of the songs on the record album "He Lived a Good Life" tells of the gathering of Jesus' disciples. Jesus gathered about him people of differing personalities and abilities. Four of his disciples were fishermen, probably somewhat crude in their manner. In fact, Jesus called James and John "sons of thunder" because of their fiery dispositions.

Andrew, however, was very considerate of others. And Thomas exhibited courage and great loyalty, even though he was pessimistic and insisted that he find out the truth for himself.

Judas Iscariot loved money and prestige, believing that he could force Jesus to deliver himself miraculously by arranging the arrest of Jesus.

Matthew (Levi) was probably a very "cultured" person, but he was despised as a tax collector. The other Simon (the Zealot) was a member of a Jewish nationalistic party.

Philip was a timid person, and yet he introduced his friend Nathaniel to Jesus. Nathaniel (or Bartholomew) was reflective, and it was he who was open-minded enough to accept Jesus as the Messiah and to convince Philip.

In the rash fisherman, Simon Peter, Jesus saw a hidden talent of leadership. He called him Peter (the Rock), but when Simon showed his weaknesses then Jesus referred to him as Simon. According to the Gospel of John, in Peter's rashness he drew a sword and cut off the ear of one of Jesus' captors. Three times Peter denied Jesus, which Jesus knew he would do. And yet, despite Peter's faults, Jesus saw the leadership potential in him.

Jesus' decisions about the disciples were based on his ability to recognize the true worth of people. He looked beyond the surface and saw the depth of truth that God placed within each.

Jesus Was Dedicated to His Belief and Mission

It seems that all through Jesus' life he was met by people who did not agree with his teachings. Even when the common people were appreciative of what he was teaching, there were always religious officials who were waiting in the background, trying to find fault and trip him up.

The officials objected to his actions—everything from his plucking ears of grain on the sabbath to his claiming that he was the Messiah. The scribes from Jerusalem told the crowds that he was possessed by demons. In today's standards we would call him a rebel. Yet Jesus continued to stand up for his beliefs. He spoke with authority, as one sent by God to proclaim God's will to men, and this disturbed many of the officials. Jesus threatened established laws and ceremonies when they were unfair or fraudulent. Jesus stood for justice and would not compromise, even to escape the cross.

Through Passover week and the crucifixion, Jesus maintained his stand. When he decided to go to Jerusalem for the Passover, some of his disciples warned him against the decision. All of them were aware of the mounting resentment toward Jesus, and they felt that Jerusalem was unsafe. Jesus knew that such a trip would mean his death, but he went anyway.

In the Garden of Gethsemane Jesus prayed again, asking for God's guidance. The decision to go through what he knew was ahead of him was a hard decision for Jesus to make as a human being. So Jesus sought God's guidance. We cannot expect to be more accomplished in living our lives than Jesus was, and we cannot expect to do it without God's help. We need to ask for guidance, too.

Jesus' Death on the Cross

To die on a cross was a cruel death and was more common than we may realize. The custom was to offer a crude anesthesia to those preparing for crucifixion—wine mingled with myrrh or gall. Matthew and Mark recorded that this was offered to Jesus, but he refused to take it. Only someone with a good physique and strong stamina could have stood the physical torment that Jesus went through during his trial and crucifixion.

On the recording "He Lived a Good Life," one phrase states, "It's not supposed to end this way."[2] For teens this may seem to be an unjust ending. But consider what the crucifixion did!

Easter

We Christians are an Easter people. From early childhood we appreciate the new life that is evident in the world at Eastertime. Spring brings with it an understanding of newness and new life. The whole world waits on tiptoe, anticipating the new life.

New Life

Like an onion with life hidden deep inside,
Oft times we sleep all winter long.
Then springtime comes, and all life is new.
Our soul's window opens with a song.

We praise God, our Creator;
We praise God in spring, a time of new birth.
We praise God, Guide of our life;
We praise God this hour, all creatures on earth.

Your teen is beginning to understand some of the depth of the Easter experience. Any way that you can bring experiences of contrast between despair and release will strengthen his or her understanding of Passion week and Easter. Discuss the events that took place during the week of Jesus' death.

The term Maundy Thursday comes from the Latin word *mandare*, meaning "to command." Communion, or the Last Supper, which we celebrate on Maundy Thursday, is a meal that Jesus commanded us to share. It commemorates the last meal that he ate with his disciples.

We can call the day of Jesus' death "Good Friday" because we know what happened afterwards. The disciples were very depressed after that first Good Friday. But we live on the bright side of the crucifixion. We know the end of the story. Without Easter, our life is at a dead end. Teens need to realize that God would not let Jesus stay dead. God showed power over all that is in the world. The cross tells us that God's love is far greater than anything that we can do wrong. God can take something that appears to be as dark as the death of Jesus, and turn it into an experience as brilliant as Easter.

Jesus, for the Teen

When I am asked if I have been saved, I usually reply, "Yes, I was saved about two thousand years ago. And I have also accepted that salvation many times in my lifetime." Teens need to realize that the actual saving act happened on a cross on a hill near Jerusalem on that day that Jesus died.

In the act of allowing Jesus to die on the cross, God forgave all of our sins. We call this redemption. This does not mean that we are forever forgiven no matter what we do. Instead it means that through Christ we can draw closer to God and can therefore live a more complete life, with the Holy Spirit (God within us) guiding us. Should we slip away from that relationship with God, we can reclaim it simply by asking. But once we have experienced a true oneness with God, we have no desire to do anything that will at any time break that relationship.

This is the ever available grace that God has given us. Every time we acknowledge Jesus as our personal Savior, every time we open our lives to the leading of the Holy Spirit, every time we share our understanding of Christ with others, we are again accepting that salvation for ourselves.

A personal love for Jesus is the heart of Christianity. Simply stating, "If all the world would follow Jesus and do as he taught, there would be no more wars," does not finalize our Christianity. This is only a starting point. Teaching a world of people the meaning of Jesus' life, knowing how to apply that knowledge in today's society, and convincing the world of people to put aside personal commitment for commitment to all of the people, is as big an accomplishment as ending wars.

Separation of Jesus and his teachings can be done, but we lose the key to the teachings. His life and death were what made his teachings true. We cannot separate his teachings nor his death from himself. Jesus asked Peter if he loved *him*— not his teachings. For the teens, as well as for adults, knowing Jesus is personal and calls for a personal commitment.

7

The Bible as a Guide for Teens

More than any other book, the Bible is life. The Bible is life from early civilization. The Bible is life, as God is revealed to us. The Bible is life through the centuries. And the Bible is life in our world today. Even if we try to segregate Bible teaching from other subjects and teach "biblically", there is no effective learning unless we realize that Bible and life are wedded together.

Teens are very life-centered. If they can realize that the Bible has been helpful in life situations from the beginning and speaks to life today, then the Bible will come alive to them.

The Bible is not a book of science nor strictly a history book, but it is a book about the nature of God. It begins with a faith commitment. God was in the beginning. We are made in God's image, and God gave us the breath of life. Our faith commitment is that we are of God. Therefore this book of the nature of God and life are one.

Throughout the Bible we find divine encounters in human life. These began with creation when God said, "And now we will make human beings; they will be like us and resemble us. They will have power over the fish, the birds, and all animals, domestic and wild, large and small" (Genesis 1:26, TEV).

In the early Old Testament days God and human beings spoke together often. The divine encounters were natural, everyday occurrences. The people enjoyed an intimate relationship with God and sought counsel in all that they did. It was said that they walked with God daily. In Abraham's personal relationship with God, the identity of the Hebrews as a special people became established.

However, this relationship was forgotten by many during the long period of exile in Egypt, when the people had lengthy exposure to other religions. Intimate conversations with God were no longer common occurrences. Therefore, God's unique conversation with Moses was received with excitement, particularly when the plagues that Moses said God had predicted actually took place. During the years in the wilderness, the people continued to ask for a physical focus for God. They seemed to be unable to relate to a God who was everywhere. God had Moses make an ark in which to house the tablets with the Ten Commandments. This ark, later established in Jerusalem, became their center. Generations later, during the Babylonian exile, most of the people felt that separation from Jerusalem was the same as separation from God.

Throughout the rest of the Old Testament, prophets and priests spoke for God. Finally, Jesus came to help us understand better what God wants from us.

There are two approaches to studying the Bible, and we should use both. One approach is to study the historical setting of the Bible, and the other is to study its meaning for us today. One approach without the other gives us an incomplete study.

Historical Setting

In early childhood children learn that the Bible is a book that tells us about God, Jesus, and Jesus' friends. Often verses need to be paraphrased to help them grasp some of the meaning. Simple stories are told over and over, and children learn to love them. As the children become teens, they can begin to understand some of the historical background of the writings.

Many of the examples and stories in the Bible are quite

different from what is written today. It will help your teens to know something of the life-styles and the context out of which those stories came. Then they can better understand the stories.

As I was growing up, the story of Abraham and Isaac seemed to be about a harsh test that God gave Abraham. As a child, I was horror-stricken that my parents should ever be so "faithful to God" that they might follow such a direction. As I grew older I realized that this was not only a story that indicated the faithfulness of Abraham, but it was also a story conveying God's direction to the Israelites that child sacrifice was not acceptable. It is a story of the high value of an individual.

Young children find Noah and the ark to be the delightful story of a man who followed God's command to build a large boat and take pairs of animals on the boat in preparation for a great flood. Teens can grasp the reason that Noah and his family were spared death in the flood, as well as the concept of the covenant that God gave with the rainbow, the promise that the earth would never again be destroyed in such a manner.

There are other covenants in the Bible that teens can begin to understand. The covenants were promises between God and the people, or between God and a person. God made a covenant with Abraham, promising Abraham that he would be the father of a great people, even though he and his wife were far beyond the normal child-bearing years. God's covenant enabled Moses to lead the people out of Egypt even though he felt inadequate. God promised to direct him. The people of Israel often failed to keep faith, but through covenants God promised to continue to be with the people, no matter where they were. Christ's life was the new covenant, and we partake of this new covenant every time we accept the cup in the Communion service.

Teens need to realize that there are modern day covenants which we make and keep today. We make a covenant when we join the church, marry, and baptize children.

The 23rd Psalm is a favorite passage. However, most teens have very little everyday experience that relates to the psalm. Many of them have never seen sheep, and certainly don't know the characteristics of sheep. Perhaps their experience with other animals helps them realize how a shepherd protects the sheep from wild animals. But there are phrases in the psalm that will mean more to the teen with additional background.

The shepherd must locate the best pasture and move the sheep about from place to place. If the sheep remain at one place too long, not only will they run out of food, but the plants will be killed from being overgrazed. Shepherds in biblical times were the managers of the grazing on range lands.

Sheep will also die of thirst before they will drink from rushing water. It is the shepherd's responsibility either to find a pool of calm water from which they will drink or to dam up a stream, thereby creating still, quiet waters for drinking. For the shepherd to create these pools was actually a life-sustaining matter for the sheep.

Psalm 121 is one of my favorites, but when I first learned of the historical context in which it was written, I was disappointed. I felt that it took away from the meaning I had found so comforting. The hills have always been a source of joy to me. The author's statement about looking unto the hills came to my mind often. In reality, according to biblical study, this psalm was written during the time when pagan people built altars to pagan gods on "high places" on top of hills. In most of the newer translations of the Bible (including the Revised Standard Version, the New International Version, and the New English Bible) the first verse ends with a question mark. "I lift up my eyes to the hills. From whence does my help come?" Then follows the statement, "My help comes from the LORD, who made heaven and earth." The author is affirming that help comes from the one true God, the Creator, not the pagan gods whose altars are on the hills. The rest of the psalm is a great affirmation to the one true God, the Lord of the earth, who is our keeper, keeping our going out and our coming in from this time forth and for evermore.

The story of Jonah is one that teens often dismiss as just a big fish story. This is particularly true if we consider the historical aspect of the story to have been merely Jonah's experience with the fish. In reality, the ungodliness of the people of Ninevah was the historical setting, and the story tells us that we just won't be left alone when God has something for us to do.

Jonah was commissioned by God to warn the people of Ninevah of their coming judgment. However, Jonah did not like his assignment. He tried to run away, boarding a ship in another direction. When he finally did make his journey to Ninevah and appeal to the people, he was angry at God for being a compassionate God and not destroying the city, even after they repented. If the unusual incident of a large fish swallowing Jonah becomes the primary focus, then the true reason for the story will be ignored.

In his parables, Jesus used everyday examples. Some of those examples are foreign to our teens. People in today's cities do not have much experience with sowing seeds. In fact, even on the farms today, seeds are bought in bulk and are usually planted by machines. They are planted in such quantities that there is no concern over whether they all land on good soil or not. In Jesus' day the seeds were treasured because they were carefully saved from the previous year's crop. Every seed that was planted was seed that had been kept out of the food supply. So seed was a valuable teaching example. As the sower threw his seed, he tried to get it all into good ground, but because of the sowing method, some fell on rocky soil and some fell among weeds that kept them from growing well. The parable of the sower had meaning to everyone listening in Jesus' day.

Biblical Concepts Today

Although the Bible was written for adults and contains symbolism that children cannot grasp, the maturing mind of the adolescent can begin to think abstractly and understand some of the profound truths put forth in the book.

I have known adults who can quote every major Bible verse and answer any question with a Bible reference and yet are unable to apply the teachings of the Bible to their everyday lives. Knowing verses is helpful, particularly for quick reference. But we must realize that the verses themselves are not the faith. The verses are vehicles to explore the great teachings that are our heritage through the Bible.

In applying the biblical teachings to everyday life, we sometimes assume that the Bible says what we want it to say. We read ourselves into the Bible, instead of reading Jesus from it. Too often we pull isolated verses out of their context. We must read the total passage or story and even the situation in which the story or statement was written. This is particularly true in the letters of the New Testament, because these letters were written to specific people or groups of people who were having special problems.

Paul's directives about the Lord's Supper in the First Letter to the church in Corinth are often taken in separate pieces. Verses 28 and 29 of chapter 11 are sometimes explained as a statement that we should not consider taking Communion unless we have totally confessed all of our sins. However, if we read the complete passage, from verse 17 to the end of the chapter, we will see that Paul was reprimanding the Corinthians for making pigs and gluttons of themselves at the meal that they were eating together in memory of Christ. "When you come together, it is not the Lord's supper you eat, for as you eat, each of you goes ahead without waiting for anybody else. One remains hungry; another gets drunk" (vv. 20-21). At the close of the chapter he tells them to "wait for each other" and to eat at home if they are hungry (v. 34).

This understanding of the context in which these verses were written does not take away our need to confess our sins to God. It removes "confession" as a kind of entrance exam and makes the act of confessing our sins a constant requirement, whether or not we are partaking of the Lord's Supper.

Although we want our children to appreciate the Bible and learn to use the book itself as a tool, we can teach the truths of the Bible without reading directly from the Bible. I had a woman tell me, "My grandfather taught me more about the Bible than anyone else. And he taught it every day, seldom reciting a Bible verse in the exact words."

Her grandfather was a produce farmer, and Liz often went with him to the farmer's market. She sat beside him as he sold tomatoes and beans and turnip greens. As he weighed up a scale, he would turn to her and say, "Now, Liz, you put the greens on the scale until it hits the pound mark. And then you reach over and take a little bit more, and you put that on. The Bible tells us to give a full measure."

The truth in the biblical concepts shines through in our lives. The best way to help teens reflect on their biblical foundations is to state specifically when the truths you are using are from the Bible. Unless we relate these concepts in everyday life to the Bible, verbally, the teen will never realize the wealth of help that is in the book.

Encouraging adolescents to rewrite some of Jesus' parables themselves, in today's situations, can help them to look for the real meanings and apply them in everyday terms.

Gifts of God

Debbie liked to run. One day she heard about a marathon race and decided to enter. She sped through the street, easily pulling ahead of the others. After a few blocks, racers passed her by. Each block, she fell behind and finished last.

Losing the marathon did not dampen Debbie's joy for running. She learned that by running a slower more even pace she ran farther in a shorter time. After many months of work she entered another marathon and won.

In the same school a boy named Robert thought, *If only I could stand up in class and talk, then I could be a leader.* But each time he read a report his knees wobbled and words stuck in his throat.

One day Robert stood before his mirror. Aloud, he asked himself, "Why can't you say what you want to say in front of other people?"

Every day he talked to himself in the mirror. Soon he became accustomed to his own voice and volunteered for the next assignment. Watching himself, day after day, he read the report aloud. When the appointed day arrived, Robert imagined himself in front of his mirror and read the assignment.

Two years later he stood before the student body and thanked his classmates for electing him president.

A third student, Carole, wrote a short story for an English assignment. The teacher read the story to the class and said, "Some day this student will be an author." Carole dreamed of autographing books.

But when the next writing assignment was given, Carole decided that the short story was so easy that the new assignment needed no work. She watched TV all evening and quickly wrote the story before class the next morning. Consequently, she received a poor mark and decided that writing was too hard.

Soon the words did not seem to write themselves as they had before, and Carole failed.

This story is a modern-day parable similar to the one that Jesus told in Matthew 25:14-30. Take time to read it now in your Bible. Matthew said that God gives each of us different abilities, and if we use our abilities they will grow. But if we do nothing with them, even the abilities that we have will be taken away.[1]

Combining Historical Setting and Today's Meaning

The understanding of the historical setting and the application of biblical concepts in today's life are both important for teens as they study the Bible. Because we are not familiar with the names, places, and circumstances of the Bible, it is helpful if we study the Bible with other Christians. Our understanding and appreciation are deepened by group study with people of various backgrounds and understanding. Listed below are five questions that teens will find helpful in directing their thoughts in both group and private Bible study. These questions are suggested in a retreat resource by Rev. Steve Clapp.

1. What do you know about the background of the passage?
2. What did the words mean for those to whom they were addressed?
3. What does the passage say to you about your relationship with God?
4. What does the passage say to you about your relationship with other people?
5. If you took the passage seriously, what changes would you make in your life?[2]

Learning to Use the Bible

One of the best gifts that you can give your teen is a working knowledge of the Bible. By this, I mean helping the young person to become acquainted with the mechanics of finding his or her way around the book.

Many churches give their students a Bible at the beginning of the second or third grade. Most churches at least have Bibles available in the classrooms for the students and help the students learn to use them, particularly finding the chapters and verses of various books. However, even if your child attended each Sunday of the third through sixth grades, he or she would probably have less than one hundred hours of practice in working with the Bible. Additional time for becoming thoroughly familiar with with Bible is needed.

Most Bibles have a few introductory pages that explain the background of the particular version and some of the mechanics of the book. There are also several self-instruction books available on the market for learning to use the Bible. However, one of the best ways to do this is to read together as a family, each reading from his or her own Bible or taking turns with the family Bible. Since many adults are lacking mastery of the Bible, this can become a family study. Teens appreciate your trying to improve your skills, and they will realize that improving our grasp of the Bible is something that we must do continually. The check list that follows will help you determine some of the skills that need work.

_____ Use the Contents to find any book in the Bible.

_____ Realize that the Bible is divided into two major parts: the part that was written before Christ and was used by Christ in his teachings, and the part that was added by the Christian church and tells about Christ and about his followers after he died.

_____ Realize that the "books" of the Bible are like a library of books; they were written at various times, over many years, and by different people, but they were inspired by God.

_____ Know the eight different groupings of books: law, history, poetry, and prophets in the Old Testament; Gospels, history, letters and revelation in the New Testament.

_____ Know the difference between books of similar names, such as 1 and 2 Chronicles and John and 1 John.

_____ Understand that the introductions to the various books tell about when they were written, by whom, and for what purpose.

_____ Be able to find a chapter in any book and any verse in the chapter, even when the verse does not begin at the beginning of the paragraph.

_____ Understand the use of the colon, semicolon, hyphen, comma, dash, and the word "through" in the Bible references.

_____ Be able to find the parts of the verse that are indicated when the letters a, b, or c are used in Bible references.

_____ Be familiar with other study helps that are printed in a specific Bible and be able to look for the footnotes that give the helps.

_____ Find maps that are in the Bible and have some working knowledge of how to use them.

You will notice that I have not included memorizing the books of the Bible in order. I feel that this is important, but I also realize that for some people rote memorization is almost impossible. We do want to stress that we work with locating the books of the Bible frequently enough that we can recognize that particular books come before or after other books. This can be even more effective than memorization, because it does not require repeating the whole list in the mind in order to find a particular book.

There are additional reference books that help us in our study of the Bible. Some libraries will have Bible dictionaries and concordances. The Bible dictionary gives brief descriptions of various words, such as "Israel," "darkness," "shoes," "Luke," and so on. It helps with developing a knowledge of the background of Bible times as well as understanding the meaning of words as they are used in the Bible.

Some Bibles have small concordances in the back. In a complete concordance you can look up any word that is used in the Bible, and it will list every place that the word is used. This helps particularly when you know parts of a Bible verse but cannot recall its entirety nor location.

Of additional help will be Bible commentaries. There are one-volume editions and multivolume editions. These are more likely to be in church libraries, or perhaps your minister has one you can look at. The commentary gives the writer's viewpoint about particular passages.

Development of the Bible

Your teen's appreciation of the Bible will be enlarged if you help him or her realize how many years of heritage went into the Bible and how it came about. The Bible began more than three thousand years ago. There was no written form at first. Stories were passed orally from generation to generation as the families sat around the campfires or went about their daily activities. We call these stories "traditions." The Bible began with these oral traditions.

Gradually parts of the Bible were written down. About two centuries ago scholars realized that the Old Testament Scriptures came from several earlier sources and had been compiled into one writing. These original complete sources are lost. The two primary sources are designated as the "J" and "E" Documents.

The "J" Document is believed to have been the first written narrative. It is dated 950 B.C. Scholars attribute it to a Judaean who was living in Jerusalem. The time of his writing was a time of optimism for the Hebrews, and most of his writings carry an optimistic tone. The author used Abraham, Jacob, Joseph, and Moses stories to establish a great national pride in Israel. This source is labeled "J" because it uses the term *Yahweh* (Jehovah) for God.

The "E" Document is believed to have come from northern Israel and uses *Elohim* (diety) for God. It contains the occasions when God appeared in more symbolic or mystical ways, such as dreams, rather than in face-to-face direct contact.

These various sources cannot be easily distinguished in the King James and Revised Standard Versions of our Bible. However, an earlier version, the Moffatt Bible, uses italics for "J" and brackets to indicate "E" when it is helpful to distinguish between the two sources.

It is believed that the first part of the Old Testament to be written was a song which the people of Israel sang when God helped Moses find a place to dig a well. The song is found in Numbers 21:17-18, and is called "The Song of the Well." Another early writing was the Song of Deborah (Judges 5), probably written around 1150 B.C.

Deuteronomy was the first book of the Bible that was accepted as holy. It was a scroll of laws found in Jerusalem about 621 B.C. The first five books of the Old Testament, or the Law, were accepted as holy in about 400 B.C. Although Amos is believed to have been the first book of the prophets that was written down (about 750 B.C.), there were earlier prophets. Their teachings were remembered and recorded later, and the people had accepted the books of the prophets as holy by 200 B.C.

The additional parts of the Old Testament are called the Writings. They include Psalms, Proverbs, Job, Ruth, Song of Solomon, Lamentations, Ecclesiastes, Esther, Daniel, Ezra, Nehemiah, and First and Second Chronicles. These were accepted as holy after Jesus had died in A.D. 90.

Because the followers of Jesus expected him to return at

any time, they did not write his teachings down right away. Actually, Jesus' statements that began, "but I tell you," were the beginning of the oral tradition of the New Testament. Of the twenty-seven books in the New Testament, twenty-one are letters written to churches or individuals. Paul wrote at least nine of these letters between A.D. 50 and 63. It is believed that they were the first written books of the New Testament. The other letters were written after Paul's, perhaps as late as A.D. 150. The four Gospels and Acts were written between A.D. 70 and 100. Mark is believed to be the first of these recorded. The one apocalyptic book in the New Testament, Revelation, was written about A.D. 100. There were other writings, and by A.D. 393 churches had divided opinions as to which were to be regarded as holy. The bishops met at Hippo and agreed on a list of books. In A.D. 397 the bishops of the church gathered again at Carthage, a city in north Africa, and accepted the list of writings compiled by Athanasius as the canon (or standard) of the Bible, the list of books believed to have been inspired by God.

Bible Translations

In Jesus' time the Scriptures were learned by repetition. Very few people could read and write. Until the codex (or sewn) books were made, about 100, B.C., the Scriptures were written on scrolls. Until the printing press was invented in A.D. 1450, the Old and New Testaments were both copied carefully by hand.

It was only after the invention of the printing press that many copies could be made economically. Then it became important that the Bible be translated into a language that the people could read.

The Old Testament books had been written in Hebrew, the language of the people at that time. Many Jewish people today still read the Old Testament in Hebrew. As the Jews moved to other lands, they adopted the primary language, and so the Scriptures were translated into Greek. This first translation was made in about 250 B.C.

The language that Jesus spoke was Aramaic, a form of Hebrew. By the time the New Testament Scriptures were written down, most of the Christians spoke Greek, and so the books of the New Testament were written in Greek. During the time of the early church, the Romans controlled most of the Greek world, and so the Bible was then translated into Latin, the language of the Romans. A monk named Jerome completed the first acceptable translation in A.D. 405, after twenty years of work. His translation was in the language of the common people then.

Latin translations were used for many years. Latin had been made the universal and only authorized language for biblical translation in an effort to protect the true text of the Bible from mistranslation. Translation into the common language was forbidden. During the thirteen and fourteen hundreds people began to want English translations. A group of scholars at Oxford University in England, under the direction of John Wycliffe, translated the entire Bible from Latin into English, finishing about A.D. 1380. The hand-copied translations were prized and read. Most of the church leaders opposed this translation, however, and burned all the copies that they could find.

Although the first printed Bibles were in Latin, Martin Luther translated the Bible into German, his common language. These were printed for the people.

At about the same time, William Tyndale decided that an English translation from the original Hebrew and Greek (instead of from the Latin) was necessary. His translation of the New Testament was printed in A.D. 1525. Copies had to be printed in Germany and smuggled into England, because the English bishops and the king were opposed to their distribution. Tyndale was killed before completing the Old Testament. However one of his helpers, Miles Coverdale, completed it and printed the first Bible that was entirely in English in A.D. 1535. Soon afterwards, the king changed his mind and asked Coverdale to translate a new Bible to be placed in all of the churches in England. It was much like Tyndale's and was called the *Great Bible*.

As the English language changed, people began asking for different versions of the *Great Bible*. And so in the early sixteen hundreds the church leaders requested that King James agree to a new official version. The resulting King James Version was a revised version of Tyndale's translation, using the common words of the people of that time. It was published in A.D. 1611. Although it took some time for it to become popular, for several centuries it was the most popular version of the Bible.

One of the characteristics of the King James Version is the use of the pronoun "thee" for God. When the version was written, the word "thee" was a personal form of the word, in contrast to the formal "you". The use of "thee" personalized the Bible and made it more readable by the common people. Since then our language has changed, and we use "you" more commonly than "thee." Therefore, "thee" has a more distant meaning now.

Several new English versions of the Bible were published, but no one version was used widely until a group of American scholars completed the Revised Standard Version between 1946 and 1952. In recent years even more versions have been published, and a committee of scholars work to keep the Revised Standard Version up to date with our changing language. There are now books published with several translations of the New Testament side by side on a page so that a reader can compare various stories and writing styles.

Personalized Bible

It is best for adolescents to have their own Bibles. A Bible is to be used, not forbidden because of its holiness.

A young man from a very religious home began religion classes in a nearby college. His mother had always insisted that the Bible be kept only on a certain table in the living room, and anyone reading not only had to be sure that his or her hands were washed but also had to sit in a particular chair. When the young man was required to treat the Bible as a text book in college, he had difficulties. His mother had taught him to worship the Bible instead of worshiping God, and he could not use it as a tool for study.

There are some Bibles that we want to handle very carefully and take extreme caution not to damage. These are usually heirloom Bibles or Bibles that were special gifts from specific people. But we need also to have what I like to call a "working Bible." The pages need to be heavy enough that the writing does not "bleed" through. Bibles should be for our use, not forbidden and considered too holy to use just anywhere.

Encourage your teen to mark passages and even make notations in the margins of his or her Bible. Suggest that he or she develop specific marks that can be placed beside a verse(s) to indicate a reaction to the verse. Georgianna Summers, in *Teaching as Jesus Taught*, suggested that we place an exclamation mark (!) for ideas that we find exciting, a question mark (?) for those ideas that need clarification, an upward arrow (⬆) for anything that seems to tell us, "Do this," and a downward arrow (⬇) for the message "Stop doing this."[3]

Reading a passage in more than one version or translation of the Bible helps us to think through just what the verses mean. If you can buy an additional translation, invite your teen along on the shopping trip. Before leaving home, select certain passages that you appreciate and be prepared to read them in the various translations. See which translations seem to relate the meaning that helps you to understand the passage. Consider exchanging translations with a friend in order to study several of them.

Bible Study Groups

Bible study groups for teens can take on various formats. One of the best ways to begin a Bible study group is to start with the mechanics of using the Bible. Learning how to use additional resource books can also be a part of this study. This might be a good once-a-week experience for the summertime. Perhaps it can follow a breakfast together.

During this study, group members will naturally have some questions. Adolescents are full of questions. Use these questions as opportunities to locate cross references and become familiar with the resource books. Begin a list of questions for more in-depth study, and add to the list each time there is another question. After the teens have had time to learn how to use the Bible and have a beginning background on additional resources, they can move into a more specific study of the particular areas that they have questioned. At this point it will be best if the adult leader can be a clarifier, one who takes a neutral stand on controversial subjects and encourages the teens to do their own searching and questioning, arriving at their own answers.

We hope that our teens will grow to appreciate the Bible as

we do. However, it is important to remember that the process of developing individual identity during the adolescent years naturally leads to a resistance to much that parents value and hold dear. When you meet with resistance, simply state your need for using the Bible, and in everyday occasions share some of the insights that you have gained. Much of the material in this chapter can be shared with your teen. However, become familiar with it and let it be a natural part of your daily conversations.

The Bible is our guide and our resource book, our inspiration for life. God is ever in it and speaking through it. Without the Bible, our Christianity would have no foundation.

Where to Look for Help in the Bible

1. When you are worried — Matthew 6:25-34
2. When you want to be important — Mark 10:35-45
3. When things go wrong and you are tempted to blame other people — 1 John 1:8-9
4. When you are lonely or fearful — Psalm 23 or Hebrews 13:5b-7
5. When someone you love dies — Romans 8:35-39
6. When it is hard to do what you feel is right — 1 Peter 3:13-17
7. When you have trouble getting along with people — Romans 12:14-21
8. When you are too discouraged to try again — Philippians 3:13-14
9. When you feel your parents are unfair — Hebrews 12:5-11
10. When you have a fight or disagreement with someone you care about — 1 Corinthians 13:1-7[4]

8

God's Will in the World

A Time for Everything

There is a time for everything,
and a season for every activity under heaven:

a time to be born and a time to die,
a time to plant and a time to uproot,
a time to kill and and a time to heal,
a time to tear down and a time to build,
a time to weep and a time to laugh,
a time to mourn and a time to dance,
a time to scatter stones and a time to gather them,
a time to embrace and a time to refrain,
a time to search and a time to give up,
a time to keep and a time to throw away,
a time to tear and a time to mend,
a time to be silent and a time to speak,
a time to love and a time to hate,
a time for war and a time for peace.

What does the worker gain from his toil? I have seen the burden God has laid on men. He has made everything beautiful in its time. He has also set eternity in the hearts of men; yet they cannot fathom what God has done from beginning to end. I know that there is nothing better for men than to be happy and do good while they live. That every man may eat and drink, and find satisfaction in all his toil—this is the gift of God. I know that everything God does will endure forever; nothing can be added to it and nothing taken from it. God does it, so man will revere him (Ecclesiastes 3:1-14).

The writer of Ecclesiastes gave us an insight into the partnership that we have with God. The writer sees it as a partnership in which we play a strong role, but in which God has control at all times.

Being a teen in today's world is more complicated than it has ever been. The more we learn about life and the scientific workings of the world, the more we try to take control of all of life and explain the whole universe scientifically. In years past there were questions of "Why?", just as there are today. However, these questions were usually answered by Christians with Paul's statement, "For now we see in a mirror dimly, but then face to face. Now I know in part; then I shall understand fully, even as I have been fully understood" (1 Corinthians 13:12, RSV).

Today, not only do we try to explain the "why's" scientifically, but we also stress an attitude of self-sufficiency and consider ourselves deficient if we admit that we do not understand something within our life pattern.

According to the Scriptures in Genesis, we are made in God's image. Yet we are not all-powerful, with control of all things. Instead, we have the responsibility to be caretakers of God's creation. We need to study in order to understand better the workings of the universe, even though we can never know the answers to all of the "why's." This position of partnership with God may be better understood today if we think of it as a "middle management" position. In Philippians, Paul gave us encouragement that we can do all things through God; he did not say that we can do all things ourselves.

As we saw in the first chapter, teens are involved in the task of discovering the answer to the question "Who am I to God?" A part of doing this is understanding our relationship to the world that God made. In this chapter you will find tools to nudge your teen's inquiring stage of faith and a description of opportunities to do so. These opportunities will be in the everyday world of nature and social relationships.

Observe Nature

About five years ago I began holding seminars and speaking to parents about ways that they can help their children and teens develop faith. I was convinced that we do not take hold of everyday opportunities to look for God at work in the world, and so I made a concentrated effort to look for every situation that might help us develop a closer relationship with God. I found that my own faith grew. I began seeing God in the world around me: in nature, in people, and in relationships between myself and nature and between myself and other people. This effort opened a totally new understanding of God for me. It brought God from the "untouchable" and "unapproachable" to the everyday and here-with-us-now. I believe that the best way we parents can help a relationship between God and a teen to grow is first to seek the relationship for ourselves. We will have to "stop and smell the roses," so to speak.

In the rush of today's life, we may ignore the everyday evidence of God. Consider the power that God has put in one blade of grass that pushes up through asphalt. The growing power within a seed begins when certain requirements are met. In science courses teens learn about the power within a tree seed; the seed will take root in small deposits of soil in a crevice of rock and force a large boulder to break. The schools cannot teach them that this power comes from God, but we can express this ourselves.

In art courses teens work with symmetrical designs. There are many symmetrical patterns in the world. One wing of a butterfly is a mirror image of the other. Most insects are symmetrical. Leaves, seeds, fruits, and many shells are symmetrical. The snowflake has radial symmetry, with identical rays or lines extending from the center.

One of the greatest marvels of God's creation is the intricacy of a spider web. God has given the tiny spider the ability to weave a design so intricate that it would take a person many tedious hours to duplicate it in lace. And no matter how hard we try, we can never duplicate the majestic beauty of a spider's web full of dew, sparkling in the early morning sunlight.

> God has set eternity in our hearts;
> yet we cannot fathom what God has done
> from beginning to end.

Teens enjoy night hours. There is a wealth of experiences in the night that can draw us closer to God. At night most of the noise of traffic is dulled, and new sounds emerge. In the quiet you can hear sounds of insects or animals. There are also sounds that reflect the inventive minds of people, such as the hum of a factory during the night shift. Even the products of our minds stem from God, because God has also set eternity in our minds. Listening to the subdued noises helps us to center on God, our creator. This listening is a form of worship, whether we label it such or not. We become more aware of God's presence.

One winter when our children were teens, we cut down a large oak tree that had died. It took weeks to cut up all the wood from that tree. In fact, the huge tree lay across our back yard, and we cut on it as we had time or need for firewood. Before the grass began to sprout in the spring, we concentrated on cutting the rest of the log and stacking it for fuel for the following year. Suddenly it dawned on us that all of those stacks of wood had come from one small acorn. God created the world in such a manner that something as small as an acorn could produce enough fuel for us to burn in our fireplace for two winters.

We began to reflect on just how that tree came about in the first place. The rings on the tree indicated that it had lived for well over one hundred years. Our home was built on a ridge in a wooded area, and quite possibly some squirrel had buried the acorn for its winter rations. Have you ever noticed just how many nuts a squirrel buries in the fall? God gave the squirrel an instinct to bury many more acorns than it needs, and many are left to become tall oaks.

I had a true worship experience one year as I stood in a grove of young sand pines and looked at a cone, which was tightly closed to protect the seeds within. My forester husband explained to me how the cone remains tightly closed against animals and birds until after it has been exposed to excessive heat. Should the woods burn and destroy every other seed on the ground, the cone would protect the seeds, even though it might be charred. After the heat has come and gone, the cone opens and releases the seeds, which are ready to sprout and reproduce. God's infinite plan includes jack pines, southern pond pines and sand pines—all of which have such cones. Plants are vital for our life. Without plants to manufacture oxygen, we could not breathe. It is a worship experience to realize God's eternal plan to provide protection for some seeds in case of fire. We cannot fathom all that God has done from beginning to end.

Change

In our church we have a table in the hall that we call the Interest Center. It is located where everyone can enjoy it: adults, teens, and children. Each week families of the church take turns bringing in different items to remind us of God's plan for the world or to give us some insight into our Christian life. One week there were seeds and plants from sprouted seeds, with the hulls of the seeds discarded around the plants. Seeds must die in order to provide new life. This reminded us that Jesus' death gave us new life, a new type of life that brought us closer to God. If Jesus had not been willing to die, if he had compromised in his mission, then we would not have our Christian faith and the relationship with God that the Holy Spirit brings to us today. Our own life in Christ must be much like a seed. We must be willing to let our own desires be used, as the center of the seed, to produce the mission that God has for us.

When we teach children, we often use the caterpillar as an example of how life changes. Children can thrill at the change, but they cannot grasp the abstract comparison to that change which comes to us through Christ. Teens and adults can truly marvel at the transition.

There is a delightful little book by Trina Paulus called *Hope for the Flowers*. The story is about a caterpillar who tried to climb to the top of a caterpillar pile. Stripe, the caterpillar, joins a column of crawling caterpillars, climbing to he is not sure where. He continues to climb, hoping to find something special in life. In the struggle he meets Yellow, and together they puzzle over the value of climbing to the top, when they don't even know what is at the top. They give up the climb, but Stripe cannot let go of his desire to reach the top and once again starts to climb. Yellow remains on the ground and soon learns that she must give herself up to being in a cocoon and spend some time as if she were dead in order to change into a butterfly, which is what she is meant to become. The rest of the lovely story tells how she helps Stripe realize that he, too, can become a butterfly, and that he can then be special, flying instead of climbing on top of and over other caterpillars.

God works in our world through change. It is evident all around us. Some changes are subtle and others are dramatic. In some, as in a seed or a caterpillar, we appear to die. But from that death comes new life.

Many times the changes in the world interact. Consider the progressive growth of a forest.

When a yard or any piece of land is left dormant for a period of years, a plant succession transforms the area from open space to deep evergreen woods and finally to a mature grove of hardwoods. In the first stage of the process you will notice various seed-producing grasses and weeds. The field mice and rabbits tunnel through the clover and grasses, and, if the property is in a rural area, deer graze there, too. Birds foraging for grass seed drop additional seeds and berries and new species appear. Soon there are thistle, wild astor, sorrel, plantain, blackberry, and poke-weed. In two to three years the broom sedge often crowds out the other weeds. This thins the ground cover, producing the ideal condition for pine seeds to germinate.

Within a few years the pine seedlings appear about the remaining forage, and an evergreen forest has begun. In about ten years the pines dominate the area, reaching about fifteen feet in height. They shade the ground and deposit a mat of pine needles, making the soil too acid for most other plants. For several years the pines dominate the area, and the red squirrels, jays, warblers, and nuthatches thrive.

As the pines mature, they lose their lower limbs, competing for the light. The understory is now open for hardwoods. Since pine seedlings require sunlight, they offer no competition for the maple, gum, and poplar seedlings which do well in the shade. The seeds of these hardwoods are brought in by the wind. In this forest small animals begin to browse and build their homes.

The pines naturally thin themselves, being susceptible to disease. The rotting pines attract insects and fungi, and soon the woodpeckers move into the forest. As the pines fall, they join the rotting leaves on the ground to become the "sacrifice layer" of soil (humus). The pine, leaves, insects, etc., give up life to form a rich soil. This is God's plan to recycle a stump.

Forty years after the first pine seedlings, the hardwood forest is on its way, with trees large enough to show a blaze of fall color under the pines.

About sixty years after it all began, the forest stands thick with hardwoods, several pines looming above the canopy of branches, like sentinels standing watch. The early hardwoods (maple, gum, and poplar) dominate the growing generation of oaks and hickories that were planted almost totally by squirrels.

The hundred-year-old forest has seen a succession from weeds to pines, then the hardwoods seeded by the wind or planted by the squirrels. As the sentinel pines die off, there is an understory of dogwood, redbud, and other smaller trees indigenous of the area. Short woody plants and low, shade-loving shrubs develop, and a mature forest begins to reproduce itself each fall, by dropping its seeds into the decaying matter beneath.

And so, watching for vacant land can be an opportunity to observe the continuing creativity of God. The weedy field or deserted yard may be spotted as the first stage. Look for small evergreens peeping above the weeds and guess the length of time God's re-creation process has been at work. Then find the dense pine forest, and you have located the next stage. With a little practice you can guess the age of the hardwood forest by spotting a sentinel pine above the canopy.[1]

God has set eternity in our hearts;
> yet we cannot fathom what God has done
> from beginning to end.

God and Science

Most often when we think of God and science, the age old debate arises: Did God create the earth or did it just happen by accidental circumstances? Personally, I cannot understand how anyone can fail to believe that God is the Creator, whether creation was accomplished in six 24-hour days or over a long period of time. If it was by accidental circumstances, then the elements that accidentally came together to form the earth had to have come from somewhere. What is essential is that God is the source of all life. If not God, then where else is our source?

There are varying views on creation. Share your own view with your teen and state that there are other people with other views. Remember that he or she is in the process of developing a faith independent of yours. That faith may hold some of the same beliefs as yours, but it is not truly his or hers unless it has been questioned, tried on, and adapted personally.

Help your teen realize that no matter what the beliefs on creation, all Christians believe that God is the source of creation. Our main goal is to have experience with the Creator, because that is why God made us. This is faith.

Science is from God, not opposing God. And nature is God's laboratory. Everything shows the wonderous works of God, from the lightning of a thunderstorm flashing across the mountains to the tides that lap the seashore.

The family is a good place to enjoy hymns of praise to God— praise for the wonder of creation, for the gift of free will, and for Christ to guide the way. Buy a hymnal and use hymns as devotions, as poems before meals, or as poems of joy. Read the words without music sometimes, and think about the meaning of each word.

Dependable God

God is a dependable God. In the science of mathematics we can rely on the dependability of God. Each time that we multiply five times nine we can be sure that we will have forty-five.

I was working with some young teens one evening. They were drawing pictures to illustrate talents that God had given them. The pictures were to be dedicated to God in a worship service. As one of the boys watched others drawing figures of themselves singing, or helping a friend, or playing a sport, he said, "I don't have any talents." I asked him if there wasn't a class in school that he was better in than another. He said, "I'm pretty good in math, but that's not a talent. That's just school!" I told him that I believed that math was a talent God had given him.

I truly believe that an ability in math is a strong talent. To understand the intricate laws of mathematics that God has set up in the world is as much a God-given talent as playing a five-page piece of music or running for a touchdown. Accountants have told me that one aspect that attracts them to mathematics is the dependability of an equation. And that dependability came from God. Those mathematical laws are set fast in our universe, and we can be sure that they were established by God.

> The heavens are yours, and yours also the earth;
> you founded the world and all that is in it.
> —Psalm 89:11

Each year spring will follow winter. If it were not to happen, then God would not have placed the buds in the trees to lie dormant through the winter. About a month before the branches burst forth with leaves, I become restless, checking the trees for any change. The buds are there, but they have not grown. And then, following a few warm days, the buds begin to swell, and I know that God's dependability is surely with us. I turn down the furnace for the first truly warm day and rely on God's sun for warmth.

I look to the sky and see the flying "V" of the geese, returning from their flight south. Their instinct is of God, and they rely on that instinct to guide them.

In Israel today there are olive trees that were growing when Jesus walked the roads. Some plants grow quickly, such as mushrooms, and others grow more slowly. But each grows according to the plan that God set in creation, and that plan is dependable.

We can predict the tides to the minute. The stars are set in their courses, and they follow those courses so perfectly that sailors can guide their ships by using the stars to determine their position.

Teens are beginning to learn about the early morning sun's reflection in the air, which gives everything a pink hue. Children worship God through the beauty of such circumstances. The worship of the omnipotent God can be even greater for teens and adults when they recognize that God made the system of the world that makes possible such reflection of light in the air.

Science explains the cycle of the seasons and the changing of the leaves, but the reason is of God. The reason is God's control over the universe.

Teens understand the scientific operation through which the roots and leaves gather the nutritional needs for the tree and process them for growth. When we recognize God as the source and reason for the whole process, our appreciation of God is enriched.

Cause and Effect

Teens naturally question why we have natural disasters and why there are diseases with no known cures. We can help them realize that God has set up specific, dependable laws in our universe. These laws govern a cause-and-effect course of events.

A study of the history of medicine can be an exciting venture if we realize that all knowledge of medicine has potentially been in the world from the beginning of time, and that God made our minds with an ability to seek out and grasp that knowledge, to work with it, and to use it to control diseases. Some diseases we have conquered, but others are still waiting for the proper understanding of cause and effect within the natural world created by God.

We also need to establish the causes of some diseases for which humans have been responsible. At times our decisions and choices have created diseases new to us because we have not yet learned the results and long-term effects of some of our actions. If God had not made the world in this manner, we would be only puppets. But we are made in God's image, with our own wills, and we must learn how to direct those wills in accordance with the laws set by God.

When I consider the revolutionary discoveries of Louis Pasteur in the mid-eighteen-hundreds, I marvel over the way that God established our interrelated world. Before Pasteur's discovery, women avoided hospitals for the birth of their babies because too often the mothers who used the hospitals suffered illnesses themselves and died. With an understanding of bacteria, the hospital personnel began to realize the need to wash their hands after examining one woman before moving on to the next. Unknowingly, they had been spreading the germs of one patient to another. All of this was within the make-up of God's laws, but we had not yet learned how to understand those laws and to work with them.

We have developed better understanding of the laws of weather in recent years. Today we can predict many storms or at least recognize the conditions that often produce such storms. We have learned that by destroying the vegetation at certain locations, we create circumstances that result in flooding during excessive rains. This knowledge about the weather has saved many lives.

From a study of the Chattahoochee River in Georgia, I learned that the harvest of oysters in the northeastern part of the Gulf of Mexico is dependent upon the trees of the mountains of northern Georgia. Should all of the trees be cut, there would be no nutrients from the falling leaves to wash down the river and into the Gulf of Mexico for the oysters. The balance of nature is set by God's scale.

What will we learn in the future that will change our understanding of science? When science cannot explain something today, the discovery of a new law in the universe may explain it tomorrow—and behind it all is the reason, God. We need to use the talents given to us, following God's guidance, and we then can move forward into unknown realms of science.

Death

Death is a part of the change in our world. As Christians, we believe that death is a process of moving from one existence into another. Ask a teen if he or she remembers what it was like to be in the womb before birth. There is no conscious recollection. No baby willingly leaves the comfortable womb. Experiments have shown that placing babies into warm water immediately after delivery lessens the trauma of birth. This indicates that the baby can feel the difference between the conditions in the womb and those in the dry atmosphere.

Just as we cannot recall the conditions before birth, our transition in death is something we cannot understand until we experience it. We are unknowledgeable about what to expect, but we have learned in this life that God's plan for us is all-wise and all-loving. And as we grow in our relationship with God, then we know that we can depend on the plan after death.

In the teens' effort to piece together the different impressions of the world that they receive, they will wrestle with what seems to be a lack of "fairness" in death. A peer who seems to have the whole world ahead may die young, while another may continue to live in a body wracked with pain. A drunk, driving on a public street, may walk away from an accident without a scratch, while a young child in the other car suffers brain damage for life.

In an effort to explain the unexplainable, some Christians label these circumstances "God's will." With such explanations, the teen is likely to decide that he or she will have nothing to do with a God who will "zap" someone who is productive in life and leave another who seems to be useless. This approach puts God into a position of moving us about on a playing board like pawns in a chess game.

Rather, we are created in God's image. We are created with wills of our own, and with those wills we can decide our own actions. We can be creative or destructive. Because we have the individual will, then in the circumstances resulting from our decision, the death is the will of God.

Leslie Weatherhead, in his book *The Will of God*, defines God's will as having three parts: "The intentional will of God means the way in which God pours himself out in goodness, such as the true father longs to do for his son."[2]

Created in the image of God, we were intentionally given free will, ". . . because man's free will creates circumstances of evil that cut across God's plans . . . there is a will within the will of God, or what I call 'the circumstantial will of God.'"[3]

Yet we are not left with the empty statement "That's just the way it is!" We can use the circumstantial will of God and grow in our relationship. If we follow God's guidance, working to fulfill the original plan, then we will accomplish the ultimate will of God.[4] We will have a greater life in Christ than God had even planned in the beginning.

As Christians our concept of death includes eternal life. We see that life is more than physical bodies. Teens are dealing with abstract thought now and can begin to see the soul as that part of the self that loves, that aches for others and chooses to help them, that sorrows, and that praises God. We believe that after death God's plan for us is far greater than anything that we can conceive. Realizing this, we do not grieve for the person who has died.

However, we grieve for ourselves, for our loneliness and for others' loneliness. God experienced grief through Jesus. I remind you again of the story of Lazarus in John 11. Jesus learned of Lazarus' illness but postponed going to him because he intended to raise Lazarus from the dead. But when Jesus went into the house and saw Mary and Martha's grief, he wept with them, although he knew that Lazarus would live. Jesus placed his stamp of approval on the grief process that God has built into us.

The first stage of shock helps us move through the immediate mechanics of dealing with a death. It is later, when the shock wears off, that the second stage of acute grief sets in. Then we often experience restless sleep, anger, disorganization, loss of appetite, and withdrawal from life. If we remember Paul's statement—that everything fits into a pattern for good if we love the Lord—then we can move into the third stage and begin rebuilding our lives.

I have met Christians who concentrated on the joy for the person who had died, and did not recognize Jesus' tears at Bethany. These people eventually suffer the second stage of grief, although they may not openly acknowledge it. Then they can create guilt for themselves, believing that any grief is unchristian. Sometimes they think that they have lost their religion. It is important for us to help our teens realize that the hurt that comes with grief is natural. It is a process that God built into our lives as a sort of vent. It releases us and prepares us for the task of rebuilding, so that we can continue our relationship with God.

Personal Relationships

The making and breaking of friendships can be traumatic for teens. It is important for your teen to realize that there are different levels of friendships.

In a lifetime we may have only two or three friends we can actually call *close*. A common feeling and understanding flows between close friends. They can reveal things to each other that would kill any other type of friendship.

Good friends are more prevalent, and the relationship offers great rewards. Good friends enjoy many things in common. They thrive on the give-and-take of conversations on mutual interests. They share their excitement and joys as well as their sorrows. A good friend may develop into a close friend, given the right circumstances.

Casual friends are many. They develop with neighborhood locations, business associates, and through other friends. They are the wildflower garden of life; growth depends on the location and climate. They may become good or close friends.[5]

There are seasons of friendship. Each person grows in his

or her own particular pattern, and at times friendships develop that are beneficial to both parties. However, teens need to realize that sometimes letting go of a friendship is the best way that he or she can grow.

Developing friendship brings joy, but it also brings responsibility. A close friendship doesn't just happen, and if it is to remain close, it must involve caring for the other person as much as for yourself.

Jesus taught that we should love even our enemies. The New Testament was written in Greek, and we use the word "love" to translate four Greek words (*eros, philos, charis,* and *agape*), each a different form of the verb "to love." *Eros* is the highly emotional love that teens most often think of. *Philos* is a love for another as a fulfillment of self. *Charis* is the love that God shows for us, even when we do not deserve it. Sometimes this is translated as "grace." And *agape* is our response to God's love as shown for other people. With an *agape* love we will not tear down other people but will build them up, lifting each individual's importance as God sees him or her. This is the love that Christ had for Zacchaeus and the woman who anointed his feet, and this is the love that he felt for each person in Jerusalem when he said, "I would have gathered you to myself, as a hen gathers her brood."

When a marriage relationship breaks down, teens can suffer from grief as well as the parents. The grief is over the broken relationship, and it can carry all of the stages of a grief over death. Don't hide your grieving from your teen, but realize that he or she is viewing the broken relationship from a different perspective than yours. It is important for the teen to realize that although the relationship is no longer healthy between the parents, the parent-teen relationship may be possible with individual parents. Peer groups of teens in the same situation can be helpful for your child. Many mental health centers offer weekly seminars that will help children understand what is happening and how they fit into the new relationships. Such groups can also help children to build up self-esteem that often suffers in a divorce.

The People of the World

The world of teens is an expanding world. They are becoming aware of the people in other countries. Our "instant picture" society has given them windows into most of the world, and they often do not like what they see. We tell our teens that God created us all equal, that we are all brothers and sisters under one Creator. Yet any teen who watches the evening news on television knows that the child with the thin, drawn face and extended stomach, crying for food in a Third World country, has not been treated as equal. They try to put the different parts of their world together, and the pieces do not fit.

As teens grow older, they become more aware of the wars that break out between countries. They are particularly aware that they may become involved in a war someday, and they begin to weigh their attitudes, wondering if their convictions for or against the war are stable. They ask, "Is war really the will of God?"

Each person must make his or her own personal decision concerning wars, and each must weigh that decision again and again, based upon the circumstances and guided by prayer in searching for God's will. Just as God does not "zap" the young child with a drunk driver, I cannot feel that God creates hatred within peoples so that we have wars. I believe that this evil is all a result of God's will that we have individual wills of our own. Sometimes those wills are misused and are not in line with God. Sometimes hatred is germinated. Each person must make an individual decision whether war can be God's will in *those* circumstances. And we must use any circumstances beyond our control, and with God's help bring about the ultimate will, aligning our lives with God.

It is important that we develop sensitivity in our youth. Christ was sensitive to the needs of others. Christ was aware that his people were oppressed, and yet he did not gather armies and fight the oppressors. He encountered individuals and responded to their personal needs. He helped Zacchaeus recognize how he could change. Because of that change, Zacchaeus gave half of what he had to the poor and restored fourfold to anyone he had defrauded. When the woman anointed Jesus with an expensive ointment, he recognized her need to minister to him in that way and did not reprimand her for it.

Jesus was sensitive to the person behind the actions. He

saw all of Jerusalem, and wept for what he could not do for them individually. For Jesus was a personal Savior. He was personal to those who responded to him, and he was dedicated to the personal well-being of all individuals, wanting to gather them together "as a hen gathers her brood under her wings."

By giving us a free will
God has set eternity in our hearts;
yet we cannot fathom what God has done
from beginning to end.

9

God's Personal Challenge to Teens

Faith is more than believing something regardless of the evidence; it is daring to do something regardless of the consequences.[1]

In the adolescent years teens are just beginning to feel some control of their lives. It is hard for them to commit themselves to something so totally that they can let the chips fall where they may. This is particularly true when their peers do not submit to the same commitment. If we truly commit ourselves to Christ, then we follow him no matter what the consequences.

There comes a time when we need to say to teens, "Yes, we have nurtured you, we have loved you, and we have taught you. But there is still something more about life over which you, without God, have no control. There is an impulse to do evil. But, with God, you can sidestep that impulse and use your talents and gifts to follow in the Christian way."

Deciding to follow God's guidance is sometimes termed "salvation." A teen may have made the decision to follow Christ before he or she enters the inquiring stage of faith. At that point in their faith journey, when they question their beliefs, they may feel that they are "going back" on their decision. Help your teen realize that searching is healthy. I had a college professor once who said, "If your faith cannot be questioned, then you had better find another faith." Any true faith can stand up under the questions, and beliefs should be lifted up and reexamined periodically.

In the past we have placed emphasis on the important one-time decision for faith. Saul's conversion is a famous example of a one-time conversion. At that time Saul became Paul, a totally changed person and important to the development of the early church.

Yet, Timothy was also important to the early church. He was one of Paul's closest companions. In 1 Corinthians 4:17, 1 Timothy 1:2-18, and 2 Timothy 1:2, Paul referred to him as his much-loved child or son. In 2 Timothy 1:5 (RSV), Paul said, "I am reminded of your sincere faith, a faith that dwelt first in your grandmother Lois and your mother Eunice and now, I am sure, dwells in you." Timothy was raised in faith. Paul recognized the importance of being well established in the faith within the family.

If one-time decisions are stressed as a goal, then sometimes there is a let-down after the emotional experience. We need to be inclusive of teens in the total fellowship of the church from the beginning. Relationships with adults who are continually growing in new faith directions help the teens realize that their decision is an important step, but it is a part of a continual faith growth process as we journey through life.

Feel free to share your spiritual growth with your teen. Discuss your own questions and the answers that support your faith. Even when we admit that we have not found an answer, the teen may be pushed into searching for himself or herself. I had one adult tell me that although she wished that her parents had been more of a Christian example and had been able to raise her in the faith, she is thankful that they pushed her into searching out her own faith by saying, "I hope you find a god to help you, because I sure haven't." Look back over your own faith journey and see how far you have come. Realize, and help your teen to realize, that the only dumb question is the one that you don't ask.

The teen needs to recognize that religious choices are not just "what I'm comfortable with." But rather, religious choices are "what I see as true." The youth's great question should be, "Am I reflecting the image of God to others, or is this mirror obscure?" Most teens are ready for the challenge to be a committed disciple.

Affirm Giftedness

Each of us has individual gifts, and our uniqueness comes from the different gifts and how we use them.

A Bag of Tools
by R. L. Sharpe

Isn't it strange
That princes and kings,
And clowns that caper
In sawdust rings,
And common people
Like you and me
Are builders for eternity?

Each is given a bag of tools,
A shapeless mass,
A book of rules;
And each must make,
Ere life is flown,
A stumbling-block
Or a stepping-stone.[2]

The teen's recognition and use of his or her giftedness is an esteem-building part of acknowledging the grace of God, as the chart on page 11 indicates.

Stephen D. Jones, in his book *Faith Shaping*, suggests five points about giftedness for youth today to consider.[3]

1. *We have more than we think we do.*

Teens are concerned about themselves, about whether they are acceptable or worthy. Jesus tells them that their giftedness is far greater than they can imagine it being. Adolescence is the age when they are just beginning to uncover their talents.

2. *The more we give, the more we have.*

The more we give our talents, the more developed they are and the greater service they can be for God. Recall the modern day parable "Gifts of God," in chapter 7 of this book. The teens who continued to use their talents were given even greater ability. But the one who did not develop her talent soon lost what she did have.

3. *We've got to know what we have in order to give what we have.*

Our talents continue to rise to the surface, but sometimes we have to take inventory. We must keep on growing in self-awareness and discovering our abilities. That is God's way.

4. *Our own gifts need to be called forth by others. They recognize our gifts before we do.*

Youth are usually willing for others to call forth their talents. However, we must know the youth in order to be able to do this. Knowing them and searching positively for their talents can help us bring out the best in them.

5. *The only way to use effectively what we have is to volunteer what we have.*

If the youth have a pride in their abilities, then they will come forth and volunteer themselves. The most effective way that I've found in helping people feel natural about volunteering their services is to ask, "How can we help *you* to be in ministry?" I have had people tell me, "It is so nice to have someone ask me to be in ministry and to give me the opportunity to evaluate where I can be most effective, instead of just being asked to do a job." As adults we can set an example by offering our gifts in volunteer service and verbalizing to the youth that these gifts are God's, and we are only returning them.

A PROCLAMATION OF GIFTEDNESS
A Paraphrase (Ephesians 1:3-10, 18-19)

PRAISE BE TO GOD, who has freely given us more than we need to put our lives into proper order.

We have been fully endowed and gifted!

God decided at the beginning of the world that all human life would, by definition, have purpose and value and be worthy of His Complete Love.

Our future and our destiny are to be discovered as we recognize ourselves as sons and daughters of God.

In Christ, that which imprisons us can be liberated.

Through Christ our mistakes, our limitations, and our guilt will be completely forgiven.

God has been lavish with human beings, giving us full wisdom and insight.

God has even made known to us the hidden purpose in creating this world: namely, that the universe, all heaven and earth, might be brought into unity and wholeness because of the sacrifice of His Son, Jesus Christ.

I pray that you might be given the inner vision to know:

First, the future to which God is calling you;
Second, the vast resources God offers to share with you if you
   believe in Him;
Third, the power within us that God can make available.[4]

God's Plan for Teens

Teens "follow the crowd" for acceptance. It is a way of satisfying the need for self-esteem. We can help them satisfy the need for self-esteem through service to Christ and to others.

Discovering how and where we fit into God's plan is sometimes painful. Peter had such a problem. When Jesus first met Peter, he saw the hidden talent within and declared that on Peter he would establish his church. Peter loved Jesus; however, when it came right down to using his talent, Peter denied Christ three times, and each time he felt sorry. The book of Acts records Peter's leadership role in the church. If Peter could overcome his difficulties and become the strength of the church, then others can too.

For a Christian, vocation is beyond career. A career is a job, a job that has some direction. But a vocation is even beyond that for a Christian. Our vocation is our response to God's call to fulfillment. If our career can fit into that call to fulfillment, then the career is a part of our vocation. The vocation is working within God's plan.

The youth learns to make and do in the world. But this requires discipline. There are many things we can make in this world. But how can we make use of what we can do, for God?

Yes, discovering how and where we fit into God's plan is sometimes painful. A friend of mine was told by a professor in college that she had a real "gift" as an artist, and she was advised to move to another city in order to study art and develop the talent. The professor even impressed upon her the belief that not developing such a talent was a sin. When she told the professor that she had family obligations that made it impractical for her to move, he simply said, "Leave them!" But she remained with her family and taught art privately in small groups. Soon she discovered that as she helped others with art, they were able to use the experience to process their faith journeys. Now she is attending seminary and further developing her talent for counseling, which she might never have known had she followed the professor's advice. As she phrases it, "I might be in counseling now myself had I not made the decision to be faithful in the relationships to which I had committed myself."

All parts of our lives must fit together in service to God if we are to be in vocation—not just our career. Being in vocation with God means that at this time, and in this place, and in order to follow God's will, this is what I am to do. Our church has just developed a new program for mothers who affirm motherhood as their current career. They are looking at their life vocation of service to God and saying, "At this time, and in this place, in order to follow God's will, I am a full-time mother." This does not negate a change of career in the future.

Teens need to look ahead to future careers, but they also need to realize that their current careers as students, their part-time jobs in stores and fast-food restaurants, are a part of their over-all vocation for God.

Realizing that throughout their lives today's teens are likely to have several career changes, we need to help them learn to atune themselves to God's calling in their vocation. I have a counted-cross-stitch picture of a tree with green apples, and on it is the statement "The green apple of June is right for the season." This reminds me that there is a season for everything in our vocation of serving God.

Parents' Growth

The questions that the teens bring up and share with you may uncover unresolved areas in your own faith search. Don't avoid these areas and don't let them embarrass you. Face the questions, together with your teen.

I spent many years debating the divinity of Christ within my own heart and mind. When I was asked my views, I simply stated that I knew that some people had one view and some another, and that I was still struggling with mine. I knew that Jesus had come to show us what God is like, but I reasoned that the prophets had done that also. Then someone suggested to me that Jesus also came so that God could actually experience just what it is to be completely human. This gave me a totally new insight into Christ. And this insight came when my children were in their teen years. My son and I were struggling with some of the same concepts.

A living faith constantly looks for new ways to grow. Our deeper relationship with God matures throughout life, until we die. And then, as Christians, we believe the ultimate in relationship with God comes about. Rather than entering a physical "heaven" where we sit back and rock, gloating with power and prestige over those who are not in heaven and looking at streets paved with gold, we believe that we will move into our "middle management" partnership and realize more fully our common goal with God. We will enjoy a fellowship with God in which our "sin" of breaking that relationship no longer exists. We will have a personal vocation, with God as the center.

Notes

Chapter 1

[1] John Larsen, "Family Counseling: A Resource for Adolescent Problems," *Marriage and Family Living* (December 1981), p. 21.
[2] G. Temp Sparkman, *The Salvation and Nurture of the Child of God* (Valley Forge: Judson Press, 1983), pp. 109-112.
[3] Merton P. Strommen, *Five Cries of Youth* (New York: Harper & Row, Publishers, Inc., 1974).

Chapter 3

[1] Stephen D. Jones, *Faith Shaping* (Valley Forge: Judson Press, 1980), p. 87.
[2] *Ibid.*, pp. 29-30.
[3] James W. Fowler, *Stages of Faith: The Psychology of Human Development and the Quest for Meaning* (New York: Harper & Row Publishers, Inc., 1981), chapters 15-21.

Chapter 4

[1] James J. DiGiecomo, "The Religious Needs of Teens," *Marriage and Family Living* (October 1981), p. 8.
[2] G. Temp Sparkman, *The Salvation and Nurture of the Child of God* (Valley Forge: Judson Press, 1983), pp. 30-31.

Chapter 5

[1] Charles and Ann Morse, *Whobody There?* (Nashville: Upper Room, 1977).
[2] Quoted by Albert D. Belden, *The Practice of Prayer* (New York: Harper & Row, Publishers, Inc., 1954), in *The Art of Personal Prayer*, by Lance Webb (Nashville: Abingdon Press, 1962), p. 11.
[3] Webb, *The Art of Personal Prayer*, pp. 32-33.
[4] *The Book of Common Prayer*, The Protestant Espicopal Church of the U.S.A. (New York: James Pott & Co., n.d.), p. 534.

[5] Thom Schultz, "Sometimes I Doubt", *Group* (February 1983), p. A-19.

Chapter 6

[1] James Allan Francis, *The Real Jesus and Other Sermons* (Valley Forge: Judson Press, 1926), p. 123.

[2] "He Lived a Good Life," Good Life Music, 4008 Aldrich Avenue South, Minneapolis, MN 55409.

Chapter 7

[1] Delia Halverson, "Gifts of God," *Accent on Youth* (Summer 1981), p. 35.

[2] Steve Clapp, *The C-4 Journal* (C-4 Resources: Sidell, Ill., 1981), p. 58.

[3] Georgianna Summers, *Teaching as Jesus Taught* (Nashville: Discipleship Resources, 1983), p. 49.

[4] *Ibid.* pp. 91-92.

Chapter 8

[1] Delia T. Halverson, *Helping Your Child Discover Faith* (Valley Forge: Judson Press, 1982), pp. 40-41.

[2] Leslie D. Weatherhead, *The Will of God* (Nashville: Abingdon Press, 1976; first copyright, Whitmore & Son, 1944), p. 14. Copyright renewal © 1972 by Leslie D. Weatherhead. Used by permission of the publisher, Abingdon Press.

[3] *Ibid.*, p. 24.

[4] *Ibid.*

[5] Delia Halverson, "My Friends: Who Are They?" *The Church School* (May 1978), p. 28.

Chapter 9

[1] *Asbury College Daily Walk* (Atlanta: Walk Thru the Bible Ministries, Inc., December 1981), p. 17.

[2] R. L. Sharpe, "A Bag of Tools," *Masterpieces of Religious Verse*, ed., James Dalton Morrison (New York: Harper & Row, Publishers, Inc., 1948), p. 306.

[3] Stephen D. Jones, *Faith Shaping* (Valley Forge: Judson Press 1980) pp. 76-78.

[4] *Ibid.*, p. 78.